ABIGAIL SCOTT DUNIWAY *and* SUSAN B. ANTHONY *in* OREGON

ABIGAIL SCOTT DUNIWAY *and* SUSAN B. ANTHONY *in* OREGON

HESITATE NO LONGER

JENNIFER CHAMBERS

THE History PRESS

Published by The History Press
Charleston, SC
www.historypress.net

First published 2018

Manufactured in the United States

ISBN 9781625859785

Library of Congress Control Number: 2017958372

Notice: The information in this book is true and complete to the best of our knowledge. It is offered without guarantee on the part of the author or The History Press. The author and The History Press disclaim all liability in connection with the use of this book.

The young women of today, free to study, to speak, to write, to choose their occupation, should remember that every inch of this freedom was bought for them at a great price. It is for them to show their gratitude by helping onward the reforms of their own times, by spreading the light of freedom and of truth still wider. The debt that each generation owes to the past it must pay to the future.
—Abigail Scott Duniway

I declare to you that woman must not depend upon the protection of man, but must be taught to protect herself, and there I take my stand.
—Susan B. Anthony

When we all see justice, we all see peace.
—Michael Franti

I hope to teach my children that everyone struggles, but it matters that you persist. No matter what. The people I write about keep going. They have faith. They work for what matters. They show up. I could teach my kids nothing better than to emulate that.

I couldn't do anything I do without the incredible support and love of my husband and children. This book—and everything I do—I owe to them.
—JBC

Contents

PREFACE

EXCERPT FROM ABIGAIL SCOTT DUNIWAY'S "THE DESTINY OF OUR REPUBLIC," OCTOBER 5, 1874

Friends, this testimonial of your presence this evening almost overpowers me. As I stand here, I look back through the dim vista of almost a quarter of a century to the days when I first landed, a young girl, a stranger in this our beautiful State, then a Territory. Then rapidly my mind flashes across the intervening years to the short time that has marked my public life. Three years ago I was almost wholly unknown outside of the little circle of my family and friends who had known me from childhood....

And it is, indeed, meet that we, their children, descendants of those hardy pioneers—ourselves yet pioneers, who have wandered across the unbeaten tracks of the Western wilds and pitched our tents upon this distant shore of the bracing and breezy Pacific—it is indeed meet that we should pause in the hurry and worry of everyday existence and drop a tear to their memory, chant an anthem of praise to their heroic patriotism, and sing a deep and solemn dirge over the graves of those who fell battling in the foremost ranks of liberty that we, their children, might enjoy the priceless boon of freedom and the peerless blessings of education and religion, which they gladly laid down their lives to bequeath to us.

It is idle for me to spend time in talking to you, my friends, tonight, about that occurrence in our history of which every American patriot in whose heart burns the fire that lights the flames of liberty has sung while chanting hymns of praise to freedom.

Women, including those representing the state of Oregon, in a suffrage march in Washington, D.C., 1913. *Library of Congress.*

But when we look abroad over our country, and see that, despite its many beautiful surroundings and glorious possibilities, there is yet so much of suffering to alleviate, so much of ignorance to overcome, so much of prejudice to destroy, so much of materialism and coarse selfishness and avarice and misery among us, we feel that there is indeed work for the philanthropist that takes on gigantic shapes and stirs the soul of the deepest and most thoughtful humanitarian to its profoundest depths.

Glance abroad over our country and you find that we have jails and gibbets, and penitentiaries and almshouses and asylums for the insane. You find, too, that we have need of these. You find, too, the wretched drunkard going down to ruin, while all manner of legalized temptations are suffered to lie in wait for the unwary, and beguile the weak into error and crime. And shall we as a people, forget these, the lowliest of God's children? Shall we cloak ourselves about with a mantle of our own self-righteousness, and, because our lines have fallen to us in pleasant places, consider it beneath ourselves to look down upon those children of Almighty God who may need our uplifting care? Shall we not rather feel that it is not beneath us to stoop to lift the fallen, to strengthen the weak, to encourage the timid, and to help the faltering upon life's rugged highway? Our country's destiny should point us not so much to our future financial greatness—not so much to grand piles of architecture, monumental structures of human greatness that shall live in the annals of history long after we shall have passed away—should point not nearly so much to our grand system of railroads and telegraphs and to everything that betokens a high state of rapid life and rapid civilization, as it should point to the necessity that the human mind shall reach out and grasp after the possibilities that are ever clustering around the humblest son and daughter of God.

We, as a people, have become so engrossed in the mad search for gain, that we have forgotten too often to look from our own fancied greatness as a Republic down into the lower strata of human life, and cast about us to see whether or not it may be possible to benefit those who are not so well situated as ourselves. And we, too, have grown so sordid and selfish, the most of us, that we are too apt to look down upon those who have been imbued with humanitarian ideas, and dared to work accordingly.

We are often told that if we would be happy, we must be good; and while I know that there is much truth in this idea in the abstract, yet let us cast about us and see if there is not much human destiny that is attributable not so much to man's want of goodness as to his want of happiness; and then, having seen that the reason why so many people are not good is because they are not happy, let us see if there is not a reason why they are not happy which the humanitarian can reach; and, reaching, apply it to those whom he may have opportunity to benefit. It is very easy for the man or woman who is surrounded with everything that makes life pleasant and agreeable to be good. We naturally feel, when the world goes smooth with us, and our neighbors treat us well, and our friends respect us, it is very natural, I say, for us in circumstances like these to feel that after all we are walking in about the right way, and then we are thoroughly satisfied with ourselves.

Now, let the same human being who is thus so good, genial, pleasant, comfortable, and affable, be suddenly deprived of house and lands, of home and family and kindred, and be thrown out upon the cold charity of the world, penniless, suffering and destitute; such as is the case with nine-tenths of the people of this great Republic who go first into the pathways of crime. Let us suppose that one of these good men or good women who never has been seriously tempted, never has seriously gone astray, is suddenly placed in one of the worst conditions of destitution. Think you when the pangs of hunger take hold upon the vitals, when the storms of heaven beat pitilessly upon the uncovered head, when it seems that human sympathy and human agency have gone from him, think you that he would not then be very likely to break some of the great commandments which all his life before he has found it easy to live up to? I think that we too often lose sight of this consideration when we would censure those who go astray.[1]

INTRODUCTION

Cautious, careful people, always casting about to preserve their reputation and social standing, never can bring about a reform. Those who are really in earnest must be willing to be anything or nothing in the world's estimation.
—Susan B. Anthony[2]

I read in another source during research for my book *Remarkable Oregon Woman: Revolutionaries & Visionaries* (The History Press) that Susan B. Anthony detested sleeping outside so much that she would never willingly camp again. This nugget of information, so in contrast with Abigail Scott Duniway's overblown and flowery writing that I was familiar with from researching Duniway, intrigued me. That small bit of a story spurred the completion of this book about two such different women and what they did for the women of my home state—Oregon—as well as the country at large.

They were fighting for the same cause but with such different skill sets, presentation style and personality. It looked from my interpretation of her early writing about Susan B. Anthony that Abigail had almost a hero worship for her mentor. Her diary pictured her as giddy to meet her. She was pleased to share her tent accommodations. She was proud to share her state. Her pioneer experiences were trotted out both for sympathy and a sense of canny realism that added authenticity to their talks. I wish we could have captured one of their speeches on audio or video, just to have heard their cadences of speech and to see the way they moved across the podium. Despite the voluminous skirts, you can almost see Abigail prowl and stride to juxtapose against Susan B. Anthony's prim, tightly controlled movements.

Susan B. Anthony newspaper portrait, 1897. *Library of Congress.*

Now, that is all in my own imagination, since having studied the women I feel like I know them; for a contemporary account, see this excerpt from Eugene Debs in the *Socialist Woman* of 1909. Debs, a union leader who helped found the Industrial Workers of the World, visited Anthony twice in her lifetime, although they knew each other through letters and mutual friends. He wrote:

I can still see the aversion so unfeelingly expressed for this magnificent woman. Even my friends were disgusted with me for piloting such an "undesirable citizen" into the community. It is hard to understand, after all these years, how bitter and implacable the people were, especially the women, toward the leaders of this movement.

As we walked along the street I was painfully aware that Miss Anthony was an object of derision and contempt, and in my heart I resented it and later I had often to defend my position, which, of course, I was ever ready to do.

The meetings of Miss Anthony and her co-workers were but poorly attended and all but barren of results. Such was the loathing of the community for a woman who dared to talk in public about "woman's rights" that people would not go to see her even to satisfy their curiosity. She was simply not to be tolerated and it would not have required any great amount of egging-on to have excited the people to drive her from the community.

To all of this Miss Anthony, to all appearance, was entirely oblivious. She could not have helped noticing it for there were those who thrust their insults upon her but she gave no sign and bore no resentment.

I can see her still as she walked along, neatly but carelessly attired, her bonnet somewhat awry, mere trifles which were scarcely noticed, if at all, in the presence of her splendid womanhood. She seemed absorbed completely in her mission. She could scarcely speak of anything else. The rights and wrongs of her sex seemed to completely possess her and to dominate all her thoughts and acts.

On the platform she spoke with characteristic earnestness and at times with such intensity as to awe her audience, if not compel conviction. She had an inexhaustible fund of information in regard to current affairs, and dates and data for all things. She spoke with great rapidity and forcefullness; her command of language was remarkable and her periods were all well-rounded and eloquently delivered. No thoughtful person could hear her without being convinced of her honesty and the purity of her motive. Her face fairly glowed with the spirit of her message and her soul was in her speech.

But the superb quality, the crowning virtue she possessed, was her moral heroism.

Susan B. Anthony had this quality in an eminent degree. She fearlessly faced the ignorant multitude or walked unafraid among those who scorned her. She had the dignity of perfect self-reliance without a shadow of conceit to mar it. She was a stern character, an uncompromising personality, but she had the heart of a woman and none more tender ever throbbed for the weak and the oppressed of earth.[3]

One could hardly ask for a better epitaph than that. I do love contemporary accounts for how they make you feel that you really know a person. Reading an autobiography is revealing too, but it's easier to correct personal bias and have an unvarnished account that leaves out all the edges when contemporaries write about a subject.

As for Abigail, her story is also almost mythical in import and circumstance. Because she fictionalized many parts of her pioneer history, it's easy to get a sense of the toughness and mental fortitude it took to do many of the things she did. Few of us in modern times know what it is like to carve, literally, a life from out of the clay, trees and scrub. It's not exactly living in wilderness to say you don't have wi-fi in your building.

Both *The Oregonian* and *The Women's Tribune* reported on the speech Abigail made in October 1905 at the Lewis and Clark Exposition at the day specified in her honor. Randall A. Lake at the Annaberg School for Communication and Journalism at the University of Southern California has set up a website devoted to Abigail and her speeches called "She Flies with Her Own Wings." He describes her from those newspapers as "five-foot-six, stocky, possessing a 'wondrous deep contralto voice' that sounded almost Biblical, even into old age, unflagging, articulate, and assertive, she made a strong impression. She was 'a forceful, logical platform orator, with a touch of sarcasm and a dash of humor that make her arguments effective. As an impromptu speaker she has few equals.'"[4]

Other sources described her as fit when she was young, a woman who walked five miles per day for as long as she could. She had health problems, some perhaps related to childbirth and later possibly undiagnosed diabetic complications. She herself alluded to the change in her looks in some of her speeches as she got older. She certainly was able to make her point, in speech and in print, with parables, stories and linking things to the ideals of the pioneer: self-sacrifice, hard work, the greater good.

Her antagonistic rivalry with her brother Harvey Scott, owner and editor of *The Oregonian*, was fuel for many a debate and sure made great press. On June 3, 1900, an editorial in *The Oregonian* stated about the statewide suffrage petition on the election ballot: "Woman's duties lie in the home; man's duties in the outer world. Government is a subject that belongs especially to the latter range or order of things."[5]

Abigail had been concerned and nervous about this vote over the course of its campaign and wrote to her son Clyde the year before of Holman, the assistant editor: "The only thing we fear is Scott's pup, Al Holman, and Aunt Maggie [Scott's wife] has her pry under *him*. He's an *ass*."[6]

When the issue failed once again, Abigail wrote her son: "We would have won triumphantly if the *Oregonian* had not stirred up the slum and slime of the city's purlieus, causing them to throw his bilge water on his own family from the ballot boxes of White Chapel district."[7]

What a hoot! This is illustrative of her spirit. The intersection of these two women was fuel for a furious and decades-long fight for women's rights. Both women eventually went on to conquer their separate areas of the country and influence countless others. They had setbacks, to be sure, and neither of them lived to see their ultimate goal be realized. It is interesting that they faced such antagonism but not surprising in the least.

I regularly speak at events about women's issues and am asked the question regularly that I call "the big one": "Why do you write about these women? How is this stuff important?"

When I stop looking at them a little confused, because to me it's self-evident, I respond. Because I'm brain injured, sometimes I'm not all that quick to get back on my feet, metaphorically speaking.

Here's why: I'm a woman, firstly. I'm a person, more fundamentally. I have children. Even if you don't have kids, everyone loves somebody. What on earth would you do if they did not have rights? How do you learn how to help give them rights or teach them how to stand up for themselves? By learning about the lives of others who have done the same. These women were the forerunners of modern activism. Without getting political, I think I can say with certainty that we all can agree that more voices being heard is a good thing. The lives of these women are instructive in grass-roots activism in that they can teach us how to stand up for what we believe in, whatever that is. As a person who has a disability, I've benefited from activists; as a woman, I've benefited from activists; as a worker, I've benefited from them. There are more barriers to break and more ideologies to update in the future, especially for those who are still persecuted. Writing books about women in our history won't save the world.

Someone who reads about them might, though. Inspiration is a powerful thing. It fueled the women I wrote about for their entire lives. They had successes, but they did not reach their goals in their lifetimes. I feel forced to repeat myself: in their lifetime, they did not see all women get the right to vote. And yet, they persisted.

I feel lucky to have gotten to know these women through writing this book. I hope you enjoy them as much as I have.

Chapter 1

Abigail's Fight Songs

When women's true history shall have been written, her part in the upbuilding of this nation will astound the world.
—Abigail Scott Duniway[8]

Closing Campaign Song: Words by Mrs. A.J. Duniway
Air—"Ten Thousand Miles Away"

Hail to the brightly dawning day
Where the glorious Ship of State,
With men and women all embarked
To meet their coming fate,
Shall navigate the ship, my friends,
Where politicians play,
For they've taken a trip in the Government ship
And sadly gone astray.

Chorus
Then blow ye winds a-ho—a voting we will go;
We'll stay no more on the barren shore,
But hand in hand with brothers band,
We'll guide the Ship of State
Across the raging main
Of Governmental seas, my friends,
To meet our coming fate.

Good-bye, good-bye to whisky rings;
Good-bye to Government broils;
No more shall men with vote and pen
Appropriate the spoils;
For we'll navigate the Ship of State
Beside our brothers dear,
And when the breakers round us dash
We'll shun 'em—never fear.

Then blow ye winds, etc.

Good-bye, good-bye to servile work
Where wages are not known;
John Chinaman is here to wash
And sew your buttons on.
He'll cook your beefsteak too, my boys,
And darn your stockings well,
While we, like you, will legislate
And trade and buy and sell.[9]

Abigail Scott Duniway's suffragette songs, of which she wrote many, were sung at rallies and before the sometimes quite long lectures. It must have broken up the long days in a time when the whole family still came out for large public gatherings of many kinds. Often, as per usual, it was a family affair, with her daughter Clara playing the piano and performing a song Abigail had written. Abigail kind of conscripted her family into her own personal force. A family affair, indeed; Abigail's life had been focused on family from her beginnings. Much like a woman who "wants it all" today, she transformed her life through hardship and joys to be what she wanted, despite her challenges. She was nothing if not persistent.

Some of her goals from her early days as a farmer's wife were equality for women and recognition and a lessening of the work they had to do within the family and outside of it. As the unfortunate fourth stanza shows with its "John Chinaman" line, her progressive ideas did not necessarily extend to all parts of the population. That itself is not unusual for the times, nor for the social climate in Oregon, where Chinese immigrants who were systematically disenfranchised by deed and by law were noted in large numbers after the gold rush in California. From the above song's perspective, Chinese immigrants were a way to share the workload, which

A suffrage song like those sung at rallies and marches. A line in the song reads: "The whole world at least shall hear!" *Records of the National Woman's Party, Library of Congress.*

was good from the perspective of the women in the song, at least, though not perhaps entirely a humanitarian attitude. It is interesting to note that Abigail's family employed a "Celestial" as a cook for some time, and she did write favorably about immigrants at times. She later wrote several editorials in the *New Northwest* discussing the "Chinese Question" and the "Indian Question," and her views on race were hampered by separatist suffrage ideals at times, though in some of her writing it is almost as if you can see her start to shift perspective.

Her fight songs were born in a place that was far from conflict-free. The West, with its commitment to freedom, was not free for all concerned. Portland, where the family eventually settled, had been a major shipping hub since the mid-1800s, and Oregon's population was not as pristine as it would like to think given the number of laws that governed the behavior of those considered inferior. The number of women in the West jumped from 4,949 in 1850 to 20,709 in 1860 and continued to grow, as might be expected, with population expansion.[10] Chinese Americans had become the largest immigrant group in the city by 1880.[11]

With the population expansion of all classes and races, other vices increased. Portland was a place of "Shanghais," as in the origin story of female lawyer Mary Leonard, who was captured in Italy, taken to Oregon by force and lived as a captive until she killed her captor/husband and was exonerated at her trial. She passed the bar on April 13, 1886, having apparently left the infamy of the trial behind her.[12] Portland's licentious ways extended to the large number of prostitutes and brothels extant both within and without city limits. Corri Jimenez, in the article "The Red-Lights of Portland," stated that not only did the city have the first mobile brothel on a steamer mid-stream, but in addition, "as early as the 1890's Portland acquired the reputation of a 'Sin City,' centered around the area of Burnside north of the river. By the turn of the century, there were four hundred brothels of various classes."[13] To this day, it has been said to have the dubious honor of the highest number of strip clubs per person in the nation. Alcohol, and whether the battle for temperance was a useful one, was another issue that concerned Abigail, though to a lesser extent. Portland was a wild city in a land that promised more growth in the years to come. Issues surrounding women's rights, wants, needs and occupations would grow and change along with the city, state and country.

By 1871, Abigail had done well in her suffrage campaign with Susan B. Anthony. With good humor and increasing frustration, she continued her speaking campaign for many years, preferring to speak to males, feeling, like her husband advised her, that they as voters held the control over women's rights. She wrote, "Women can't enfranchise women. They may lead a man to the ballot booth but they can't make him vote for us after we get him there. If we are too insistent they are likely to get stubborn and the advantage is all on their side. Men like to be coaxed. They will not be driven."[14]

We'll keep the fire-side too, my boys,
And read your musty tomes;
We'll use the money that we earn
To beautify your homes;
We'll use the wisdom we acquire
To legislate for good;
We know that with our cause you'll stand
When we are understood.

"Shall Women Vote? No; they might disturb the existing order of things." *S.D. Ehrhart, 1909,* Puck *magazine. Library of Congress.*

The work she did in the state of Oregon was a beacon that helped change the lives of women in her world. Her manner, brusque though it might have been at times, was dynamic, and her commitment was total. Susan B. Anthony was a catalyst for her and helped them both reach new goals that affected women everywhere and continue to do so today. Visionaries like Abigail and Susan are women to be remembered.

Chapter 2

Abigail's Beginning

The day may be approaching when the whole world will recognize woman as the equal of man.
—Susan B. Anthony[15]

Abigail Scott Duniway was taught her hard work ethos and her commitment to family from an early age. This may explain the fierce love she had for her ideals; they were prized within an independent family tradition that went back several generations. Oregon Territory's growth was not haphazard. It attracted a type of immigrant inclined to use their skills to carve a life from the land, and "settlers in Oregon placed somewhat more emphasis on community than did most other Americans of the time, and less emphasis on individual gain."[16] The previous sentence could be used to describe Abigail's upbringing and family life as well—more emphasis on community and less on personal gain. The same could be true of the cause to which she devoted her life.

Abigail Jane Scott, or "Jenny," the nickname given her by her family, was born on October 22, 1834, in Groveland, Illinois, to Anne Roelofson Scott and John Tucker Scott. Groveland is still a small town about ten miles from Peoria and unincorporated, though now the town boasts considerably more residents and businesses. The first settler in Groveland Township was her grandfather. He was participating in a wave of western expansion by the Scott family going back for four generations. They came from "the edge of the frontier, moving out from South Carolina to the foot of the blue ridge in

Kentucky, to southern Illinois and then to Groveland, Illinois, the small town which Jenny first knew."[17]

According to David Duniway, Abigail's grandson, the tightly knit family was a devout one. Her mother Anne's father was invested in the Cumberland Presbyterian Church as one of its originators. Abigail Jane was the ninth surviving child of twelve. After her own mother was injured, Anne tried to take on the care of both the home she and her husband shared and the home of her mother-in-law, continuing to have babies and care for all of them: "Baby Jenny often sat on the floor, crying, a piece of bacon attached by a string to a bedpost while house flies swarmed around her."[18]

The early years of both Abigail and the rest of her siblings centered on family, minding the other children and occasional school. Later, she would write that she did not know how she learned to read or write or when her mother had time to teach her, but somehow it happened. Farm duties were, at times, difficult due to her being one of the oldest of many female siblings, with her brothers not yet old or strong enough to help as much. Abigail pitched in to take on these responsibilities.

Her father, John Tucker Scott, was an active community member and an early proponent of migrating to Oregon. He and men like him were agents for an organization called the Oregon Provisional Emigration Society, which was based in Massachusetts and whose cause was promotion of the "Oregon Adventure." Another popular expression of the time that referred to such an adventure was going "to see the elephant," which meant to be willing to undergo extremes in order to see extraordinary things.

Relatives of the Scotts migrated overland in 1847 and 1851 and wrote long letters back home. At that time, the Donation Land Claim Act of 1850 gave 320 acres of land to every unmarried white male eighteen and older and 640 acres to each married couple before December 1, 1850. It is fascinating that in a married couple, the female half of the couple owned her share in her own name. The act was modified after 1850 so that between 1851 and 1854, half of those amounts was awarded. Also of note is the fact that men who were mixed Native American and white were in fact eligible.[19]

Her mother Anne, greatly beloved, had coped with ill health and the vagaries of her husband her whole adult life, as was not uncommon due to the laws of the time. Abigail does not explicitly blame her father for her mother's death in her later writings, but she does not stint from describing bitterly the things women were forced to accept. In her autobiography, *Path Breaking*, Abigail recalls her mother's reaction at the deliverance of another baby, a girl: "I remember standing at the bedside, when another little sister came into our crowded home, and my mother said, through her tears: Poor baby! She'll be a woman some day! Poor baby! A woman's lot is so hard!"[20]

The family, large but fairly comfortable for the day, had their prosperity reversed upon the death of her father's uncle Lindsey Roleofson, a man who was given the advantages of a large school and prosperity as the oldest male sibling. John, her father, had co-signed some notes for Lindsey. His misadventures after a night of carousing, when he committed some small crime, culminated in his being whipped until death by a mob. The tragedy of her youngest son's death was thought to contribute to the death, in turn, of her grandmother. Abigail describes having seen at about four years old "half dollars resting upon [her grandmother's] partly closed eyelids and noting the extreme pallor of her clay-cold face" and not being able to understand why she did not wake up.[21]

The fortunes of the family were changed by these deaths when bankruptcy forced her father and grandfather to relinquish the family farm. She wrote of the differing jobs the family performed to make do. The children participated in spinning wool and collecting sap to make maple syrup, and she wrote of the various homes they inhabited, from a set of rooms on a boat to a small log cabin. The children looked after one another. This sometimes backfired, as when one sister fell into a cooking fire. In another instance, her brother Harvey Scott was saved from a dangerous fall into a small heating stove by his sisters. They spent long hours peeling apples and stringing the quarters up to dry and preserve for later use. When she and Harvey were sent out to plant a ten-acre field with corn, they tired in the hot sun and cut the corners by leaving a large section of the middle unplanted. They were caught the next day; John Roleofson saw to it that the error was corrected as soon as it was found out. At about nine years old, Abigail had to re-sod some lawn that had been hurt by drought, which involved hacking out chunks of damaged grasses. The day gave her a back injury that never fully healed. The family fared better and moved to a bigger home once her father, John, capitalized on the sawmill craze that was sweeping the nation and imported the first sawmill to come west of Ohio.

However, it is hard not to wonder if John, described as having an "adventurous spirit," must have had a hard time seeing the multitude of wagon trains kick up dust as they wound through their little town on their way to a better life in the West. Often, barefoot children would come to the door of their cabin and beg for coals from their fire, which Anne would give them. One of Abigail's chief pleasures was reading and writing, and as a teen, while she spent six months or so at a school, she had some of her poetry

"Yours for Liberty, Abigail Scott Duniway." Abigail Scott Duniway, bust portrait, facing right. Published between 1870 and 1890. *Library of Congress.*

published in the local newspaper. The family took in boarders for extra money as well. One of these, the Reverend Lawrence, subscribed to an abolitionist newspaper edited by Horace Greely, the *New York Tribune.* Her father did not like it and called it "incendiary," but "naturally, 'Jenny' would watch her chance, carry it off, and read every word."[22]

By March 1852, the Scotts' journey to "see the elephant" had begun. It was an arduous trip. Abigail was seventeen in 1852 when her father, John, organized the wagon train to cross the country for the land that Oregon offered. He planned their trip methodically, with cash, goods, livestock and hired help to manage said livestock. It has been written in several places, including her sisters' diary, that the hired man John was "sweet on" or "taken" with Abigail. The move necessitated selling much of what they owned. A suitor of sister Fanny bought the family's set of six Dutch plates and gave them back to Fanny, who in turn gave them back to Anne. In an uncharacteristic move, Anne hid her prize wrapped deep in the feather bed that she and Fanny would sleep on, wrapped so well that the dishes would eventually survive the trip.[23] Abigail hid her own prize of a spelling and grammar book in the bottom of her basket of sewing materials. It would later prove to be a prescient thing to have saved. Abigail's chief job was to write an account of the trip. She was charged with one line a day at the least.

The maternal head of the family, Anne, was already prone to weakness from having twelve children, David Duniway related. She and her youngest son were thought to be infected with the rampant bout of "plains cholera" that rushed through the wagon trains that year. Anne, who had experienced, in Abigail's words, "excessive maternity," died of cholera on June 20, 1852. The disease was more commonly spread by tainted water, though it could be contracted person to person. The Kansas Historical Society reports that "one Missouri newspaper estimated that along a stretch of the Overland Trail one person per mile died from the disease. Historian Merrill Mattes estimates the possibility of four graves per mile along the Platte River route."[24]

Anne's grave is along the Platte River Valley route—at some point. It was believed to be near Laramie Peak. The family buried her after her death on the afternoon of June 20. Abigail later wrote in her journal that "everything was done which we possibly could do to save her life; but her constitution, long impaired by disease, was unable to withstand the attack." Her sister later wrote that Anne was wrapped and put in a grave with stones on top, and then they covered the stones with roses. It was dug next to the grave of another person who had died in the wagon train shortly before.

A crew of archaeologists from the University of Wyoming contends that they might have found her remains in 2015. The archaeologists who claim to have dug up the grave say the soft soil near where the bones were found would make the area an ideal spot to dig graves. That claim is connected to the thought that the site was near Box Elder Springs, which is what the diary says was the actual burial site of Anne. One of the people in charge of the dig, Rick Weathermon, thinks that the condition of the skeleton combined with a curious mark on the pelvis could support that theory. Anne had given birth to a child not long before the journey. The bones of the sacrum area were marked by extreme curvature and in the center had an odd "seam."

Weathermon found notes on a primitive procedure in an old medical journal of a "'symphysiology,' where in an obstructed birth, doctors would split the pelvic bone." The operation was done to help a difficult birth and was thought at one time to permanently widen the vaginal canal to make future childbirth easier. It caused long-term health consequences for women like incontinence, pain and leg weakness.[25] It also took a long time to heal, and thus Anne's "weakness" or easy susceptibility to disease could be better understood through this lens, if it were true. He saw that the seam mark could have been from a saw. If the remains were from Anne, she had possibly foregone the month-long resting period Weathermon found was customary after such a surgery. In such a case, the Civil War–era doctors recommended immobilization for weeks with a sandbag covering the pelvic area to stabilize it. However, at the time the discovery was made, they were still unsure whether the remains were those of Anne Roleofson Scott, and ethical concerns were cited as to whom the remains belonged and if they were going to attempt to identify the bones through DNA analysis.[26]

One thing to note is that graves on the Oregon Trail were often dug in the middle of the road. Doing this might contribute to degradation of DNA material, but that was kind of the point. This practice caused the freshly dug graves to be rolled over by countless wagon wheels and stomped on by thousands of feet. It helped eradicate the scent of the bodies so that the graves escaped the notice of wolves, coyotes and other predators. The trail in 1852 was marked by many deaths from cholera and also by the number of cattle that died along the way; though in journals it was said the animals died from "hollow horn," it was most probably anthrax. Researcher Stephanie Flora states that the sheer number of emigrants was a factor in the comparatively small number of altercations in 1852 with unfriendly Native Americans, along with a treaty brokered by Thomas "Broken Hand" Fitzpatrick. There were so many travelers that any given wagon was flanked by others in front of and behind them "as far as the eye can see."[27]

The grave of Abigail's youngest brother, Willie, was dug a little over two months later, on August 27, 1852. His death is thought to have also been caused by cholera. Willie, who had been spoken of as "the light of all our lives," was four years old. Years later, Abigail passed through the area where they last saw him on the way to Boise and wrote about the experience:

> *Yonder, high above the level of the plain, under a lone juniper that, for a quarter of a century, has kept solitary guard above the "silent home of the dead," is the lone grave of our brother Willie!*
>
> *Oh God! How like a vast scroll do the long years unroll themselves as we gaze through the dim vista of departed decades! On and on we go. The previous day's journey of a quarter of a century ago is now made in one hour and a half, and there, under the shadow of the stunted trees, we mark the spot where our childish muse came to us in awful solitude, when face to face with the Death Angel, we watch the waning breath of the bright little four-year-old, whose mother and ours had been buried in the Black Hills of Wyoming just ten fleeting weeks before. As we gazed, it seemed as though an angel whispered. The spot was holy. We were glad we were alone.*

She went on:

> *Eight o'clock, and breakfast….And, in spite of the flood of memories that have filled our spirit, the body is half famished. On we go again. How the long miles unroll, one after another in seemingly endless succession. Snake River is reached long before noon. Again old memories crowd upon us. The river seems to sing a requiem to John McDonald, who lost his life in trying to recover the strayed cattle of our immigrant party, a quarter of a century ago. But John knows no desert country now. Like brother Willie, he has*

> *long been transplanted from the arid plains of earth to the evergreen gardens of God. With a sigh to his memory, we cross the river in a boat, and find ourselves in Idaho.—July 14, 1876*[28]

It was speculated in David Duniway's biography as well that John, the hired hand, was a former interest of Abigail's. He helped the family and others ford a river and was swept away in the muddy current and lost. His death, among those of her family members, must have made the journey overland a melancholy one indeed. David Duniway said the experiences on the wagon train were a powerful force that shaped Abigail's personality: "It was the apt jest at times of crisis, and the romantic spirit of youth that brought Abigail through the ordeal, sharpening her power of wit and power of expression, both oral and written."[29]

There is no mention of how she got over these losses, but they were something she pushed through in any event, presumably because she was consumed with the enormous tasks awaiting when they arrived in Oregon Territory. As David Duniway stated, it seems as if her strong will was her strength and guide.

The wagon train they were on was led by Jesse Applegate. Along with his brothers Lindsay and Charles, Jesse led the first large wagon train in 1843. That train is memorable in that a splinter group broke off to form the Whitman party, who formed the Whitman Mission. Their effort trespassed on Cayuse Indian territory; subsequently, the deaths of all the Cayuse children and about half their adults led to the Whitman Massacre and the tribe's eventual absorption into the local Nez Perce. The Applegates adjusted their routes several times before the 1852 journey, but by then, crowds and lack of access to food and water en route made the trip much more difficult.

When they arrived at their destination, first in the town of Yamhill, the family stayed with the other family members who had moved out west previously. A cold, wet winter was spent in the Willamette Valley with James, Lemuel and Lawson Scott. Abigail's father, John, used the little money he had remaining of the sum he had brought to begin a hotel: the Oregon Temperance House. Abigail (she stopped going by "Jenny" except among family once she became an adult) and her sisters still had to do the onerous tasks they were used to doing for boarders, but meanwhile, she looked for employment elsewhere.

The next spring would see Abigail as a teacher in a small school in the town of Cincinnati, later to be named Eola, on the banks of where the Rickreall River joined the Willamette River.[30] Her journal related how she used the same blue reader that had been secreted on the long trip overland to teach her students. The book, with its worn cover, was so busy with the different subjects that sometimes she would have to set a group of children on a problem and then quickly run to her own desk to read ahead and solve it.

Now only eighteen, with a lifetime of experiences and losses already behind her, she met Ben C. Duniway in the town of Cincinnati. Her snapping intelligence would have seen to it that she was quite a catch. Though clever, she had a temper, but due to her teachings, she kept her tongue mostly in check. She would not let injustice go, however, and was known to be headstrong at times.

When Ben was courting her, she made it clear that he was to court her for herself alone. Abigail would not allow herself to be a "land claim" bride, one of those whom men desperate for land married in haste for the land alone. Ben, who was agreeable to this, also consented to have the word "obey" omitted from their wedding vows due to his wife's views. They were soon installed in his land claim in the land available at the time: "Hardscrabble Farm," she later called it, in Clackamas County.

The tangled land was overgrown and not as arable as the best land that was in the area, which had been claimed earlier. They did their best and in quick succession were joined by two children, Clara and then Willis. A thorn in Abigail's side was that Ben was happy to let his bachelor friends enjoy the comforts of his home almost as often as he did. Her sister Fanny married as well, as did her father, John, but her sisters Etty and Kitty lived in the Duniway household off and on. The work, though familiar to Abigail, was incredibly hard, and the diarist put some bitter thoughts at the time down later in her biography. Her phrases make it easy for a modern-day person to imagine the difficulty of the continuous, nonstop labor and the duality of what she was being asked to do as a woman: serve and not be served.

> *It was a hospitable neighborhood composed chiefly of bachelors, who found comfort in mobilizing at meal times at the homes of the few married men of the township, and seemed especially fond of congregating at the hospitable cabin home of my good husband, who was never so much in his glory as when entertaining them at his fireside, while I, if not washing, scrubbing, churning, or nursing the baby, was preparing their meals in our lean-to kitchen. To bear two children in two and a half years from my marriage day, to make thousands of pounds of butter every year for market, not including what was used in our free hotel at home; to sew and cook, and wash and iron; to bake and clean and stew and fry; to be, in short, a general*

> *pioneer drudge, with never a penny of my own, was not pleasant business for an erstwhile school teacher.*[31]

Her mind was always active, and she read as often as she was able. They spent four years at the claim. It was enough to prove their ownership. Before they left, Abigail made an enormous accomplishment. It was one that would preface the rest of her literary life.

Still an avid reader of newspapers, Abigail was compelled to write a poem called "The Burning Forest Tree," and Ben encouraged her to send it in for publication. The poem was published in the *Oregon Argus* under the pen name "Jenny Glen," and her impassioned replies to letters about women's rights were published there as well. Those letters were signed with her full name. One such letter mentioned that Ben was content to do more of the childcare and such while Abigail did harder work, and in reply, the couple got letters directed at them abusing Ben's choice. One reader even went as far as to send him a cartoon Valentine about a "hen-pecked husband."

Abigail went on to write well-liked columns for the *Oregon Farmer*. Then came her biggest success to that date: her fictionalized account of life on the Oregon Trail. *Captian Gray's Company, or Crossing the Plains and Living in Oregon*, was published by a company called S.J. McCormick in Portland, Oregon. Oregon became a state that year on Valentine's Day 1859. The book's release arrived without the sterling reviews the author had hoped for. The consensus was that it was a thinly veiled romantic tale written by a young girl. Even so, she could be proud to have had the very first novel printed west of the Rockies. She was later embarrassed by it and said, "It was a foolhardy thing for an illiterate and half-bent farmer's wife to undertake, backed only with a few months of the most primitive opportunities for education, gathered chiefly in my childhood, as elsewhere stated, from a little elementary spelling book. I scarcely knew the rudiments of correct English speaking."[32]

In the aftermath of these writings, Abigail attended meetings by noted orators. Her attendance was not exactly usual for women of the day, and it is amusing to imagine the conversations that happened in her home before she did so. These meetings informed Abigail's sense of women's inequality under the law. The seed of her championship of equal rights for women had just been planted.

Abigail's writing was seen in several newspapers as advice columns and letters to the editor as she gradually grew more confident in her writing ability. The task her father John had set upon her, as record-keeper for the overland journey, was a skill that was to pay off.

Chapter 3
Times of Adjustment

Sooner or later we all discover that the important moments in life are not the advertised ones, not the birthdays, the graduations, the weddings, not the great goals achieved. The real milestones are less prepossessing. They come to the door of memory unannounced, stray dogs that amble in, sniff around a bit and simply never leave. Our lives are measured by these.

—Susan B. Anthony[33]

"Hardscrabble Farm" was much improved by the time they had lived there for four years, but the Duniway family left the area almost as soon as the property was lived on long enough to be claimed. The pair had survived a series of tragedies: a horrendous freak storm that literally tore their cabin down around Abigail as she protected baby Clara with her own body and the cabin's later destruction by fire as the family was visiting a neighbor. It was rebuilt, but after the claim was proved, they moved to a property in Yamhill, where at least now the men she cooked and cleaned for were hired men and not the general neighborhood.

One afternoon, the future of that farm was decided—and not by Abigail:

> *I recall one day which, like hundreds of others, was occupied to the limit. After dishes were washed, beds made, rooms swept, and when dinner was over for the family and the hired men; after the week's washing was finished and the churning done, and I was busy in an outside house picking ducks—for those were pioneer days, and even our pillows, like our stockings, were*

> *home-made—a man came up from the village to our woodpile, where my husband was at work, and asked him to become surety for a considerable sum, with interest at two per cent per month.... It dawned upon me suddenly, as I was picking a duck, that it would ruin us financially if those notes were signed.*[34]

And so it happened. The notes were signed. Abigail had no say in the matter. It was disastrous for the family. That year, the crops failed and the warehouses they stored their grain in for sale were ruined when a winter flood filled them up to the ceilings. The notes became due, and the responsibility fell to the Duniways to pay them. Abigail was, in fact, served the summons for the notes while at the farm, as Ben was away for the day. She waited until the hired hands and children had gone to bed and gave the papers to Ben. Though at first she'd wanted to gloat, she found that she could not be gleeful at the way her husband turned as white as a sheet at the news. The next day, Ben went to court and the farm was sold. They moved to the property they had left, a smaller place in Lafayette, in 1865.

Her brother Harvey Scott settled in Portland after his college career around the same time. He would become editor of the state's largest newspaper, *The Oregonian*. They had a relationship that was at times acrimonious, as both she and her brother had strong opinions and feelings about issues of the day, but Harvey would also help her family later in their lives.

Once settled, Abigail thought she might be able to take in washing or keep boarders to make extra money and perhaps control some on her own. But soon after they moved in, Ben was dragged beneath his team of horses in a terrible accident that made him unable to do much physical labor for a long time. She nursed him, and her empathy toward Ben was something, she noted in her writing, that "aroused the keenest sympathies of my being."

Given his accident and their immediate needs, they decided to start a school and converted the top floor of their home (which was still being built) to take in students. Abigail got up at three o'clock in the morning to get all the work done, food made and tend to Ben as he convalesced before the school day began. She strung sheets to make "rooms" and engaged herself to teach girls in her small school for the next year.

That summer, the family moved to Albany. The home had a small shop where Ben could busy himself, but better still, the town had a place where they could open a millinery shop. Abigail told a story about going to a local wholesale dealer, Jacob Meyer, Esq., to purchase the goods she needed to

A three-piece summer day dress, United States, 1870–74, cotton tabby. Patricia Harris Gallery of Textiles & Costume, Royal Ontario Museum. Common dress of women of the period. Abigail's dresses may have been made of finer material, while Susan's were much more utilitarian, for example. *Photo by Daderot.*

open the shop. Before contacting Meyer, she had purchased the necessary physical infrastructure for the store like bins and counters. This left her with the paltry sum of $30. When she approached him, he inquired why she wouldn't go into the debt of her friends or family. She related the tale of losing the farm that way and said she'd rather not, but she'd give him her $30 if he would lend her the $100 worth of goods until she could pay him back. Meyer sent her home with $1,200 worth of supplies. She came back and paid it out of her profit in three weeks. "My next account was for three thousand dollars, and from that day to this, I have not known extreme poverty: though I am not wealthy and never can be," she wrote in *Path Breaking*.[35]

Her conversations and interactions with women at the store were the next pillar to support her women's rights ideals. Many women were barely given the money to buy things for themselves and their children, even though they worked like draft horses the rest of the time for their families.

In 1862, interracial marriage was made illegal in Oregon. However, in 1866, the Married Women's Property Act gave women their own right to own property. Progress was coming in fits and starts for Oregon women, and Abigail was going to be a huge part in that evolution—if she would only have known it.

CHAPTER 4

A MOST AUSPICIOUS MEETING (DAY-STAR OF OUR DESTINY)

Every generation of converts threshes over the same old straw.
—Susan B. Anthony[36]

Abigail felt keenly the stories women told her as she worked in her store about injustices, and she hoped that slowly newspapers and the public would become more aware of the plight that women without rights to their own bodies felt. Men could whip their wives with impunity. One story told of a man who whipped his wife all the way home from a neighbor's house, using a black snake whip, if he thought she had stayed there too long.

The fashions of the day required freshening on a regular basis. As a shrewd businesswoman who was committed to keeping her family afloat, Abigail made every effort to keep her own stock updated. She made buying and educational trips to Portland and San Francisco often and, on one such occasion, became aware of the larger women's rights conversation brewing in the town by the bay.

Her profession as a "mantua maker," as she called her art of haberdashery, perhaps lent itself to confidences, as her store was a place patronized by mainly female customers. Certainly, she became privy to other women's stories and was deeply affected by some. In one case, she went to court with a woman when the woman was being asked to settle her late husband's financial affairs. As she was familiar with the judge in the case, Abigail expressed the woman's story to him; the woman and her

Susan B. Anthony standing in a doorway. *Library of Congress.*

children had worked to sell everything possible to fulfill their creditors on assuming her husband's debt, and the widow had expressed to Abigail that "after I've earned the means to pay the bills I can't even buy a pair of shoestrings without being lectured by the court for my extravagance."[37]

Luckily, Abigail was patronized by enough people to make a good living for her family. Relating the debt incident to her husband, Ben, their conversation seems to have finally convinced Abigail that the time for women to vote, and for all women to stand up for their rights, was ripe.

This, of course, was a boon for Abigail, whose San Francisco buying trips afforded her the opportunity to see in person the suffragists, orators and the like about whom she had read. One such speaker was Emily Pitts-Stevens, editor and owner of the *California Sunday Mercury*, which she made into the suffrage newspaper *The Pioneer.* Pitts-Stevens hired an entirely female staff and was the founder of the Women's Publishing Company, as well as being a promotor for the Women's Co-Operative Printing Union. She and one of her compatriots in suffrage, Laura DeForce Gordon, were part of the

California Suffrage Association, which formed in 1870.[38] Abigail formed a kinship with Pitts-Stevens such that the latter asked Abigail to become the Oregon editor for *The Pioneer*.

Abigail and two others, Martha Foster and Martha Dalton, formed the Oregon State Equal Suffrage Association in November 1870. The California Suffrage Association, later to be formally called the California State Woman Suffrage Educational Association, was having a convention at the end of 1870, and the Oregon society sent Abigail as its state delegate. Coincidentally, she had been planning on a buying trip to the area at that time of the year, which was rather fortuitous for her selection as delegate. While on the buying trip that winter, she stayed with friends, including the family of Republican abolitionist John A. Collins. Collins was a former socialist and co-founder of the socialist communal farm at Skaneateles, New York, and friend to Frederick Douglass, as well as other influential abolitionists.

The text of Abigail's January 5, 1871 speech to the association was printed in *The Pioneer*. It was said to be the beginning of her formal oratorical career. In her preface to the speech, or her warm-up to the "meat" of her message, some of Abigail's spirit comes through, as she describes how she came to her appointment at the conference:

> *I went about a month ago from Albany, on the Wallamett, where I live, down to Portland, in the interests of my business. When I returned, the documents declaring me unanimously elected to the coming Woman's Fair and Convention in San Francisco, and introducing me to the Society here and elsewhere in the State as delegate from the Oregon Human Rights and Universal Suffrage Association, at Salem, were awaiting me in the careful custody of my sensible husband. For, be it known, oh, carping candidates for masculine monopoly—ye men who insist that no women are dissatisfied with the existing order of things except vinegar-faced spinsters, who have been crossed out in the matrimonial market—I have a husband, a radiant daughter, and five bonnie boys; and I reverently thank the great All-Father for my husband, my daughter, and my many boys.*
>
> *The association in Oregon is poor, they told me, and could give me neither purse nor scrip; but thanks to these deft hands of mine, a month's hard extra labor at mantua-making earned my steamer-fare, and I am here tonight to rejoice with you over the era of progress.*

She began the speech:

In the name of the Human Rights Society and Universal Suffrage Association of your sister State of Oregon, and as representative of a gratified people who have eagerly watched your progress from afar, and who proudly claim you as co-workers in a righteous cause, I, their humble, but willing and active servant, come tonight to greet you....

Already, my sisters, has the day-star of our destiny dawned in the distant east, and its refulgent rays are permeating even to the remotest regions of the busy, bustling West....

The present progressive political movement, which claims the attention and consideration of the greatest minds in Europe and the East, and which many thinking men and women in California willingly espouse, has found a lodgement in the home of my adoption. And throughout the smiling valleys, hillside homes and forest-shaded habitations of that growing State, the leaven of human progress and equal rights before the law is steadily at work, enlightening the dense darkness of local ignorance, decomposing the noxious influence of selfishness, and slowly undermining the sandy foundations of the iron-bound walls of bigotry and prejudice....

Official Program of the 1913 Women's Suffrage Procession, 1913. *Library of Congress.*

> *We are not insane enough to expect a sudden overthrow of all the ills which flesh is heir to when we get the ballot. Great reforms move slowly. This is the experience of ages. But you once grant the necessary conditions under which a moral reform can become developed, and your personal moral obligation concerning that particular reform becomes canceled, you are no longer a stumbling-block in its way, and of course become fitted for the next great step in the advancement of knowledge.*[39]

The stirring speech ended with a dramatic parable in a story as told by Abigail. It was her version of a poem by Martin Farquhar Tupper called "Ellen Gray: The Excuse of an Unfortunate." It showed the lot of women and the need for change. The poem seems a perfect way to describe the plight of women at the time and served to reinforce her theory that women were hampered not by ability or work ethic but societal expectation and circumstances. Her main points in the speech were that women had two roles: as a "butterfly" or "parasite" to man or a "drudge." Much of the poem is reproduced here to show how brilliant Duniway was at stirring her audience and how she could pull the emotions of her listeners out with a story that appealed to the core of anyone who supposed to care for others. She said of this poem, recited from memory during her speech, that "it carries with it a sad moral, which I hope every woman here will heed":

The night was dark and bitter cold,
The low, dim clouds all wildly rolled,
Scudding before the blast;
Around me fell the blinding sleet
As down an unfrequented street
I went my way in haste.

I bowed my head before the storm
Across my way a prostrate form
In woman's garb was seen;
I stooped and raised her fallen head,
Was she but faint from want of bread,
Or what could all this mean?

Again I raised her drooping head,
"Have you no home or friends?" I said;
"Get up, poor creature, come,

You seem unhappy, faint and weak,
How can I serve or save you? speak!
Or whither help you home?"

"Alas! Kind sir, poor Ellen Gray
Has had no home this many a day;
And but that you seem kind,
She has not found a friend of late,
To look on her with aught but hate,
And still despairs to find…

"My heart was pure, my cheek was fair,
Ah! would to God a cancer there
Had eaten out its way,
For soon my tasker, dreaded man,
With treacherous arts and wiles, began
To mark me for his prey.

"And months by months he vainly strove
To light the flame of lawless love
In my most loathing breast;
Oh! how I feared and hated him,
So basely kind, so smoothly grim,
My terror and my pest.

"Thence forward drooped my stricken head,
I lived, and died a life of dread,
Lest they should guess my shame;
But week[s] *and months would pass away,*
And all too soon the bitter day
Of wrath and ruin came…

"They tore my baby from my heart
And locked it in some hole, apart,
Where I could hear its cry,
Such was the horrid poorhouse law,
Its little throes I never saw,
Although I heard it die…"

Her eye was fixed, she said no more,
But back against the cold street door
She leaned her fainting head.
One moment she looked up and smiled,
Full of new hope, as Mercy's child—
And the poor girl was dead.[40]

Dramatic, yes; but not all hyperbole. If a woman did not possess independent means, and few did, the only way through was to marry well, and then she became little more than a slave, according to the law and societal custom.

Ben Duniway sent Abigail a telegram while she was in San Francisco saying she was needed at home but not why. Fearing bad news, back she went home to Oregon. But she found not what she had expected: "As I had left a good housekeeper in the home and a capable manager in the store, I could think of no real cause for the telegram, except possible illness to the family; so I canceled all engagements and sailed for home, where I found no visible need for anything but the salary I had relinquished in blind obedience to what I considered an unreasonable mandate."[41]

The ire of one who had waited the length of an entire reportedly gusty boat trip to find out if her family was hurt or sick is easy to imagine. In any case, after arrival, she quickly put plans into motion. The 1870 trip had rooted a desire to start her own publishing enterprise. Echoes of a voice being heard were seen back to the days when Abigail wrote columns for the *Farmer*. She envisioned an America where women could be seen and heard as equals with rights and feelings of their own both in print and reality. In May 1871, the Duniway family moved their operation to Portland and started the *New Northwest* as a "human rights" newspaper. Her sons set type as Abigail attempted to run the rest of the paper herself. The paper was sensational in style but broad enough to appeal to many.

She was nothing if not bold. One of the most extraordinary facets of Abigail's personality, and one that she attributed to her being a true "pioneer" in spirit, was her willingness to try for what she wanted. "Leap and the net shall appear," a quote by rough contemporary John Burroughs, could have been her motto. In the summer of 1871, Abigail invited Elizabeth Cady Stanton and Susan B. Anthony, who were traveling in the West at the time lecturing, to come speak to audiences in Portland and beyond. She herself had spoken at many occasions, starting with the neighbors back at the Sunny Side farm area, when her letters to the editor and columns had begun to garner acclaim.

Stanton and Anthony had championed the "no taxation without representation" principle, encouraging women to vote and exercise their human rights, resulting in several lawsuits. They challenged the sexual mores of the time alongside the women's rights issue when they fought for Victoria Woodhull in print and court. Woodhull, one of the first female stockbrokers, had come to her position in society in a questionable way. She married a man who was reportedly a drunk and not able to support her, so she left him. She and her sister soon were the mistresses of Cornelius Vanderbilt. The sisters started a newspaper after the success of their brokerage, and Victoria was a speaker at a committee in front of Congress about suffrage, saying: "One portion of citizens have no power to deprive another portion of rights and privileges such as are possessed and exercised by themselves. The male citizen has no more right [to] deprive the female citizens of the free public, political expression of opinion than the female citizen has to deprive the male citizen thereof."

Woodhull was accused of believing in "free love" when she was involved in reporting a scandal with prominent minister Henry Ward Beecher and Elizabeth Tilton, a person from his congregation, in her own journal, the *Claflin Weekly*. Critics at the time said it was in retaliation for others' exposure of her "free-love" views, but historians have also said that she was merely trying to expose the hypocrisy of others who practiced the free-love principles and were not honest about it.[42]

Woodhull spoke publicly in New York on the subject, saying, "I have an inalienable, constitutional and natural right to love whom I may, to love as long or as short a period as I can, to change that love every day if I please!"[43] It was without doubt a jolt to the established way of thinking. Yet it is a very modern point of view. Even if Abigail later softened her support of Woodhull's very radical way of thinking, she seemed to have felt a kinship, in spirit at least, to the vociferous Woodhull.

Stanton, a friend of Beecher's sister Isabella Beecher Hooker, was articulate in Woodhull's defense and said in a letter: "We have had women enough sacrificed to this sentimental, hypocritical, prattling about purity. This is one of men's most effective engines, for our division, & subjugation. He creates the public sentiment, builds the allows, & then makes us hangman for our sex."[44]

Beecher Hooker shared the same opinion. Anthony's talks were panned in the western newspapers, while Stanton's speeches were commended. It was determined that Stanton continue back east, since she was tired out from the tour and did not want to brave the journey. Anthony, who had incurred

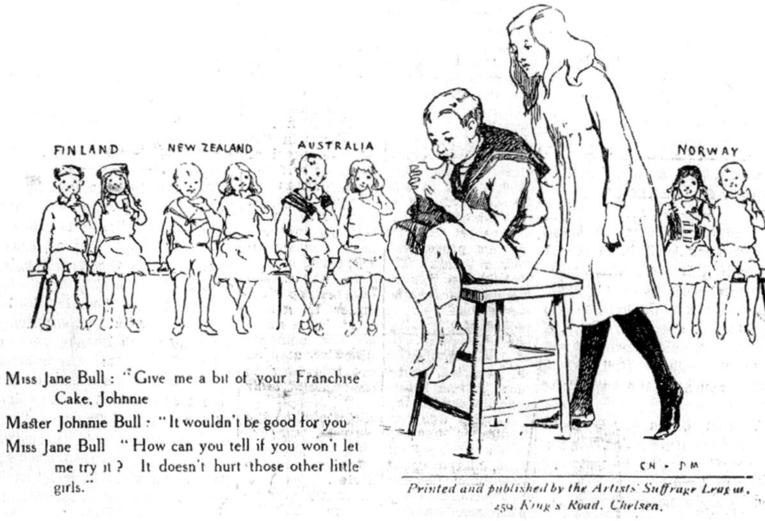

British suffrage cartoon, 1909. "Jane Bull wants a piece of John Bull's franchise cake, as it hasn't hurt girls in Finland, New Zealand, Australia, or Norway." *Library of Congress.*

debt from her publication *The Revolution* (the National Woman Suffrage Association newspaper), sailed up to Portland courtesy of Abigail to finish the remainder of her tour. Abigail had secured the plum role of co-lecturer and got a bigger name lecturer in Anthony to split the booking fees.

Cash-poor once again and ready to continue her crusade, Anthony sailed up to Portland to accept the invitation. In her book *Ladies Were Not Expected*, Dorothy Nafus Morrison writes of the seminal meeting between Abigail and Susan B. Anthony. Morrison does a great job of using the instance to shape and explain Abigail's determined, sometimes steam-roller manner:

> *The first morning the great lady was in town, Abigail donned her best suit and hat, buttoned her gloves, picked up her umbrella, and went to Miss Anthony's hotel. She was surprised at meeting "a soft-spoken, motherly looking modestly attired woman" of about fifty years, to whom she "warmed instantly." Right from the start, they were friends, and Miss Anthony approved of Ben, too.*[45]

The scene is illustrated nicely by Morrison. You can see the gutsy, audacious Abigail as if in color. She presented herself in the best style, courtesy of her own skill and her shrewd business sense, no doubt with a chapeau of the latest

Left: Susan B. Anthony and Anne Fitzhugh Miller, Geneva, New York, 1908. At their private homes and in a camp Anne created, Anne and her mother, Elizabeth, provided a place for reformers to gather; Susan stayed with them for weeks at a time. Anne later went on to be influential in women's voting rights in several states. *Library of Congress.*

Below: Two pages from the scrapbooks of Elizabeth Smith Miller and Anne Fitzhugh Miller, with a photograph of Nathaniel Schmidt, brochures, clippings and other ephemera related to the Men's League for Woman Suffrage and the Equal Franchise Society, 1910–11. *Library of Congress.*

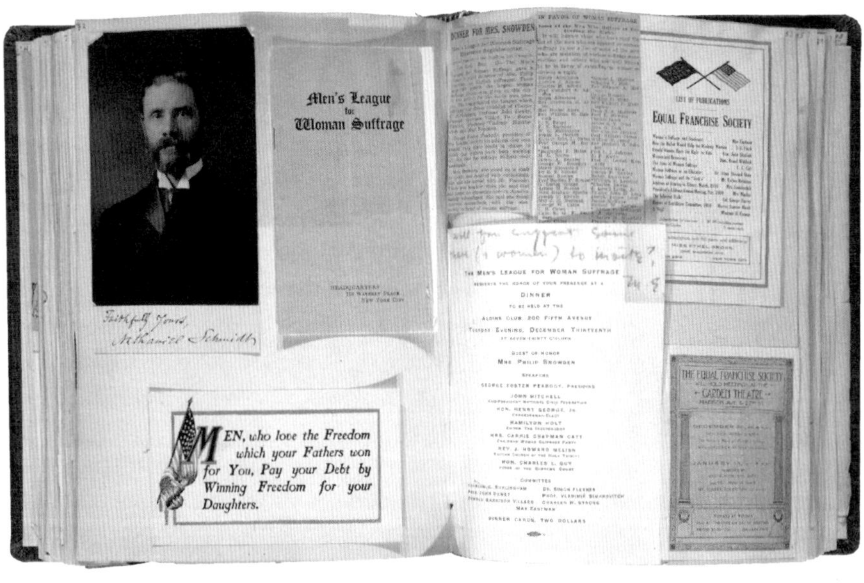

mode and highest quality. She and Anthony had spoken in San Francisco in the past when Abigail waited in line after a speech of Anthony's to comment, and they were well acquainted by letter and other brief meetings.

As for Anthony, it was auspicious timing that Abigail invited her to speak in the Northwest. Her speaking companion and long-standing friend, the much staider Elizabeth Cady Stanton, was able to distance herself from the controversial nature of Anthony's friendship with and support of Victoria Woodhull and, perhaps needing a break, went back to the East Coast.

CHAPTER 5

SUSAN B. ANTHONY IN FLUX

Marriage, to women as to men, must be a luxury, not a necessity; an incident of life, not all of it. And the only possible way to accomplish this great change is to accord to women equal power in the making, shaping and controlling of the circumstances of life.

—Susan B. Anthony, speech, spring 1875[46]

On September 1, 1854, Susan B. Anthony was unanimously elected secretary of the Whole World's Temperance Convention at the Metropolitan Hall in New York City. Temperance, or abstaining from alcohol, was linked with women's rights from the very beginning, with the two issues being treated as one. At the convention, committee member Charles C. Burleigh gave the morning speech. It opened like this:

> *This is an enterprise that recognizes no distinction of cast, sect, or nation; it is one that exhibits devotion to the great family of man. We need all the help of those who are willing to help, whatever be the sex or station of the individual, to engage in the work in which universal humanity is interested; a work which seeks the welfare of universal man.*
>
> *Our enemies never stop to discriminate—why should we? They are quite as ready to deal with one cast, one sex and one race as with another—they are just as ready to sow the seeds of poison—of moral and physical pestilence and death in one station as another, and we must meet them everywhere—we must leave no avenue undefended; no point accessible to their attack.*

Susan B. Anthony with women's rights leaders, 1896. Anthony is seated at center. In the front row, far right, is Alice Stone Blackwell. Ida A. Husted Harper is in the back row on the far right. Others pictured are Laura Clay, Annie Howard Shaw, Annie Kennedy Bidwell, Carrie Chapman Catt and Rachel Foster Avery; Winfred Harper and Mary Hayes are believed to be in the photo but unconfirmed. *Heritage Auctions.*

It is easy to see how the two points could be blurred. It is also easy to see how fiery speeches could sway hearts, and imagine how Anthony, writing down the words as they fell, could assimilate the women's cause with the case for abstaining from alcohol. After all, since time immemorial, alcohol had been a release for many in very tough times. Now with the advent of the Industrial Revolution, with drudgery taking up less of the day, people had more time to be pious.[47]

Temperance, and whether it ought to be a law, was a subject of much concern to those of the mid-1800s. It was fought with pen and oratory, even by those one might not expect. Indeed, part of the spectacle of these conventions was the personalities of the chosen speakers. At the next day of the convention, where Anthony was listening, circus proprietor Phineas T. Barnum even spoke in favor of the cause:

> *I met a friend, who informed me that there were a great many "isms" up here, and there were two classes of people present who had no right to be here. He wished to test this. In the first place, this was a World's Convention, and if there were any here who were not in the world they ought to be kicked out.* [Laughter.] *And he wished every lady and gentleman who could lay their hand upon their heart and say they had never suffered from the effects of Intemperance, either in person or in the actions of others, their friends—if there were any such, he wanted them to rise up and he would have their portraits. He did not believe that there was any man, woman, or child in the universe who could honestly say they had never suffered in any way from the effect of Intemperance....*
>
> *Now, he would like to know who was going to object to anybody speaking there against this great evil, which does so much injury to all. It was no objection to say that one person spoke on one thing, and another on other things not connected with it; for no matter what else they might talk of elsewhere, there they could all unite on the one platform and speak against an evil which has this peculiarity above all other evils—namely, that it afflicts all the world, including even the women and children. And why, then, should not the women, against whom this evil operates perhaps most injuriously of all, meet to protest against it?*[48]

Barnum, though his reputation is more inflated today, was also a respected and well-known businessman of the time. His shrewd showmanship had to have been a ticket-seller at the very least, sincere though his statements might have been. Temperance was an issue that would divide the heart of the women's struggle and one that would cause strife for the later relationship between Anthony and Abigail. In a sense, temperance was an issue that Anthony had been fighting for her whole life.

Anthony was born in 1820 in Adams, Massachusetts, and was the second of seven born to David Anthony and Lucy Read in a Quaker family that prized social justice causes. Though her family's fortunes waxed and waned, like Abigail's, she was sent to the prestigious Quaker Deborah Moulson Female Seminary until her family could not afford it after the depression of 1838. She became a teacher at an academy in New Rochelle, New York. Her commitment to social equality was such that she was out collecting signatures for antislavery petitions by the age of seventeen.

Her family moved to a farm near Rochester, New York, and it became a place where antislavery activists, including Frederick Douglass, congregated. She had met Amelia Bloomer and William Lloyd Garrison and was friendly

P.T. Barnum, between 1855 and 1865. *Library of Congress.*

with Elizabeth Cady Stanton by 1851, so that by the time she went to the States Sons of Temperance convention in 1852, the idea that she simply "Listen and Learn," as she was told to do, went against the free thinker's Quaker upbringing.[49] Her family raised "boys and girls alike," and according to how her family viewed that statement, she was comfortable speaking her mind and was raised to think she had the right to do so.

Stanton's work was crucial to how Anthony came to think. In the Women's Rights Convention in Seneca Falls, New York, of 1848, the Declaration of Sentiments, which Stanton was part of creating, read, in part:

> *We hold these truths to be self-evident: that all men and women are created equal; that they are endowed by their Creator with certain inalienable rights; that among these are life, liberty, and the pursuit of happiness; that to secure these rights governments are instituted, deriving their just powers from the consent of the governed. Whenever any form of Government becomes destructive of these ends, it is the right of those who suffer from it to refuse allegiance to it, and to insist upon the institution of a new government, laying its foundation on such principles, and organizing its powers in such form as to them shall seem most likely to effect their safety and happiness....*
>
> *Such has been the patient sufferance of the women under this government, and such is now the necessity which constrains them to demand the equal station to which they are entitled.*[50]

Anthony worked as a teacher in other capacities but was captivated by the women's rights movement and equality in general. In 1852, she was working with Stanton to create speeches, written by Stanton and performed by Anthony, and helping to write articles on things like "divorce, property rights, and temperance."[51] In 1854, she began to work on creating and having others sign petitions for women's suffrage and married women's rights to property. Also in that year, she tried to speak at the U.S. Capitol and the Smithsonian and was denied; instead, she started her campaign for suffrage in New York State.

Anthony worked and traveled by herself for a time, secure and seemingly unflappable. When she became an agent for the Anti-Slavery Society in 1856, she would have good company; her friend Stanton's husband was a staunch member of that association, and indeed, his antislavery work had brought him into Stanton's life before they married. Many of the people Anthony met in the women's movement were Quakers or Methodists, and the other slavery advocates quickly built up momentum. From 1857 to 1861, Stanton

Local membership ribbon from the Smith Miller NAWSA Scrapbooks, 1897–1911. *Library of Congress.*

and Anthony toured on an "education for women and blacks" platform and then ran an antislavery campaign through New York State. The areas they were marching through, on the Eastern Seaboard, were considered the intellectual capitals of the country at the time, and as staunch northerners, they would have a good chance of their messages being heard.

The women came to be very good friends, matched in ideals and many values, and their talents complemented each other. Reformer Anna Howard Shaw later wrote, "She [Anthony] often said that Mrs. Stanton was the brains of the new association, while she herself was merely its hands and feet; but in truth the two women worked marvelously together, for Mrs. Stanton was a master of words and could write and speak to perfection of the things Susan B. Anthony saw and felt but could not herself express."[52]

One item Anthony kept with her always was an alligator handbag. The bag and her signature red shawl became iconic symbols by which to recognize her. The bag was symbolic to Anthony in purpose, too; inside, she kept a copy of important papers, speeches, clippings and, later, a transcript of her 1873 trial. At a time when women had few possessions that they could consider their own, it was vital for her to keep these things nearby, especially as a woman who traveled often and whose schedule could be at other people's mercy. According to the Susan B. Anthony House, which has turned her family home and block into a women's history center, the purse was so emblematic that it is now reproduced to earn funds to keep up the historic site. The organization notes that the newspapers of the time printed a children's jump rope poem about the bag:

Miss Lulu had a baby, she called him tiny Tim.
She put him in the bathtub, to see if he could swim.
He drank up all the water! He ate up all the soap!
He tried to swallow the bathtub, but it wouldn't go down his throat!!
Call for the doctor!
Call for the nurse!

Call for the lady with the alligator purse!
"Mumps!" said the doctor. "Measles!" said the nurse.
"Vote!!" said the lady with the alligator purse!![53]

In 1863, Anthony and Stanton helped to gather strength for the first of the political organizations open to women in the United States, the Women's National Loyal League, to abolish slavery. They kicked off the crusade by writing an "Appeal to the Women of the Republic" that was then published in the antislavery newspaper the *New York Tribune*. The appeal was turned into a pamphlet that was an advertisement for the Women's National Loyal League convention, for which Anthony gave the opening speech. She nominated activist Lucy Stone as the president, and the league went on to collect over 100,000 signatures in support of abolishing slavery. These signatures were pieced together in two spools, placed in trunks and given to Senator Charles Sumner. The group would eventually garner over 400,000 signatures of support and count as a factor in the passage of the Thirteenth Amendment, which abolished slavery.[54]

The outbreak of the Civil War from 1861 to 1865 helped usher in a new kind of independence for women. In the South, women took on farm duties, plantation oversight, production and responsibilities as supply clerks, among other things, and made it possible for the South to continue amid the adversity of war. In the North, women did much the same. Some were nurses, like author Louisa May Alcott, who wrote about her experiences in a veiled way with her character Jo March in her novel *Little Women*. Many women and children in the North also worked in large numbers for the newly industrialized mills and factories. Unfortunately, this was often for poor pay and inferior conditions. The Working Women's Union, created in 1863, helped organize women for their own rights. Ultimately, the participation in these types of unions gave women more of a voice in the American labor movement and helped give rise to participation in feminist movements in the United States.

In 1868, Anthony and Stanton started publishing *The Revolution*,[55] a feminist newspaper, in New York City. They had lofty ideals and were pleased to be financially backed by two wealthy men, George Francis Train and the editor of the *New York World*, David Meliss. Right from the start, Stanton and Anthony pulled no punches in their frank appeal to the cause:

The Revolution*'s motto, printed on the masthead of the first edition's front page, was, "Principle, not policy; Justice, not favors." Beginning with*

Votes for Women Postcard; Color Illustration of Woman Suffrage Headquarters Building, Fifth Avenue, New York City, [November 1909]. *Library of Congress.*

> *the second edition, the following was added: "Men, their rights and nothing more; Women, their rights and nothing less." Later editions had this motto: "The True Republic—Men, their rights and nothing more; Women, their rights and nothing less."*[56]

The paper—which, ironically, had similar subscriber numbers to Duniway's *New Northwest* a few years later on the other side of the country—talked about things that other papers didn't often broach in print. That included "sex education, rape, domestic violence, divorce, prostitution and reproductive rights," and indeed, a headline in the paper's early days was "Tammany Hall and Susan B. Anthony," which certainly was not a headline one would see in the day.

One of the issues that faced *The Revolution* was a split in how reformers thought. Broadly, there were those who wanted temperance on the same platform as women's rights and were opposed to those who wanted women's rights as its own platform. Then there were those for whom race interfered. Some abolitionists were incredulous that black men would have rights before white women. The paper was criticized at every turn.

Anthony was a good editor, especially to her (mainly female and highly skilled) workers, whom she insisted on paying the high rates she felt they were owed. Coupled with her penchant for good quality equipment and the disappearance of their benefactor Train when he was jailed for his support of Irish rebels, the paper had financial trouble. Part of the problem was that Anthony was averse to using advertisements for patent medicine and alcohol, and without them, it was hard to finance the printing costs, which were roughly $20,000 per year at today's rates.

The writing of the newspaper was compelling. One article written by Stanton from the January 29, 1868 issue of *The Revolution*, titled "Save Our Girls," reasons against the use of the corset:

> *We conjure you, fathers, husbands, brothers, to give this question of woman's dress your serious consideration. Your ridicule is more powerful to set women right than reasoning on this subject, than all the sufferings they endure. No woman, though she puff like a porpoise going up-stairs, will admit her clothes are tight. You may ask your daughter, with her wasp-like waist, a dozen times a day, if her dress is not tight, and she will tell you no; and her mother will tell you that "Julia's waist always tapered just so." Do not believe a word of it. Nature never sent forth such "journey work." No girl was ever born into the world with her ribs lapped, and her vital organs*

> *all crowded together. If to propitiate some evil genius, we must cramp and trammel one sex, let the boys be the victims hereafter; it would not be half as detrimental to the race as is our system to-day.*[57]

We know today that she was correct and that it was injurious to be laced so tightly. The idea is ludicrous now, and yet still things known to cause some degree of harm are worn, such as sky-high heels. We "know better" to a large degree now but feel as if we can choose a bit more, given that such strict social and religious standards do not generally govern our society. Stanton's appeal was remarkable in that she tried to get men to listen and help sway the fashion sense and help change the standards. It is interesting to imagine whether she did so because she hoped that the men would hear the message and pass it on to their wives or because she thought the men themselves would listen and empathize and change laws that way. She details exactly why the fashion is wrong and goes further into what societal evil demands it:

> *The first step in this work is to make all women understand that suffering is not in harmony with God's will. That every pain, sorrow and wrong is in violation of his law.*
>
> *We have been taught that woman is the special object of God's wrath and curse; that the fact of motherhood, so far from being her highest glory and exaltation, is her deepest sorrow and humiliation.*

The paper spoke openly against women's mistreatment at the hands of their husbands. This was activism that had history for the pair, and it echoes the pleas that Abigail Scott Duniway was hearing on her side of the country. It's thrilling to imagine the audacity it took for Anthony and Stanton to stand up to such bullying, given the mores of the day. The Susan B. Anthony House says in its biography of Anthony: "In the 1860s Anthony and Stanton drew attention to the case of Abby McFarland whose drunken and abusive husband, Daniel, shot and killed the man she had divorced him to marry. They protested when Daniel was acquitted of murder on a plea of temporary insanity and given custody of their son."[58]

The paper was bought by someone who did not share those compunctions. Laura Curtis Bullard, corresponding secretary for the National Women's Suffrage Association and friend to Stanton and Anthony, bought the paper for one dollar in 1870. Bullard's money came from fortune that had been made from her family's successful sale of morphine and alcohol solution

Mrs. Winslow's Soothing Syrup. The tonic was advertised widely to "soothe any human or animal" and likely did so based on the qualities of its two main ingredients: morphine and alcohol. The ingredients of medicines were not required to be on the label of any medicine. It remained a bestseller until as late as 1930.

The newspaper was not as prosperous under Bullard's leadership, as shortly after she assumed responsibility she sailed for Europe with her elderly parents, and despite her best efforts at editing it from abroad, she conceded the difficulty of doing so. Especially of note was how hard it was for her to work with the resident editors, who were at that time males, and the once-weekly paper folded in February 1872. Bullard kept up her friendship with both Anthony and Stanton, however, especially Stanton, and continued to see her upon her return.

Unfortunately, Anthony had to assume the $10,000 debt for the paper. It was colossal for a single woman. The massive debt amounted to over $180,000 as adjusted for modern inflation. Partial fault for the failure of the paper was due to Train's absence and his spotty payments once he was concerned with the Irish bout for independence abroad, and part of it, too, was due to the management styles of Stanton and Anthony, but Anthony seems to have taken the failure particularly hard. She would work on the lecture circuit and tour for six years to pay off the debt. It was most likely why she acceded to Abigail's wishes to tour with her, despite her friend Stanton's refusal to continue.

In May 1871, Abigail published the first issue of the *New Northwest*. She was surely influenced by the work of the women's rights workers on the East Coast and corresponded with some regularly. That spring, she went on a trip to San Francisco. While there, she was thrilled to meet and hear Susan B. Anthony speak. In her autobiography, she characterizes Anthony as being unfairly depicted after she first met her in person: "I am proud to mention Susan B. Anthony. This wonderful woman had up to that time been an object of almost universal ridicule, being caricatured as a 'cross, cranky old maid,' an avowed 'man-hater,' and a 'dangerous agitator.'"[59]

There is a glaring tendency to name-drop in Abigail's autobiography, but that seems to have been a style of the writing of the time as well as a personality quirk of hers. She is not as effusive with praise for Stanton, with whom she had a more tepid relationship. Later in the autobiography, she goes on at length about the "grand" home of Elizabeth Cady Stanton and her husband, where Susan B. Anthony was staying. The pair was writing their manuscript of the *History of Woman Suffrage*, and Abigail all but gushes,

"The home of Mrs. Stanton is an elegant country villa, with beautiful grounds and pleasant dives, situated in the hills of New Jersey, where, at the time of our visit, the autumn leaves were aglow with a holocaust of glory."

The Victoria Woodhull issue of the early 1870s was another issue that concerned early feminists and was potentially damaging to Anthony and Stanton, as they had supported her. Woodhull was the first woman to run for president. In 1870, her name, with running mate Frederick Douglass, was on some ballots for president, but the number of voters who selected her went uncounted. When Woodhull published an article exposing Henry Ward Beecher's adultery with Elizabeth Tipton in her newspaper, she had an argument with Anthony and Stanton. It was Woodhull's stance on sexual mores that did her in. She publicly spoke about sexual topics while lecturing. She advocated a woman's right to control her own body. Most shocking was Woodhull's opinion on "free love" and the fact that she lived with her lover at the same time and apartment as she lived with both her current and former husbands. Anthony and Stanton withdrew public praise and did not mention her in their *History of Woman Suffrage*, even though besides her political ambition, Woodhull had been the first female broker on Wall Street.[60] Years later, in 1874, Anthony and Stanton were called as witnesses at Beecher's trial against Theodore Tipton.[61]

Anthony was soon to have other legal troubles. The trip with Abigail—and its offer of a free steamer ticket—could not have come at a better time for her. The woman, who was used to living with relatives, friends and in hotels, needed a new direction. The feminism movement was soon to be split into two factions.

CHAPTER 6

THE CHARACTERS OF THE REVOLUTION

It's odd that men feel they must protect women,
since for the most part they must be protected from men.
—Abigail Scott Duniway[62]

The eastern states had the largest number of females clamoring for the vote in 1871, and the northern states historically had the highest percentage of men and women who were committed to social change, if you go by antislavery activities and activists.

Victoria Woodhull continued to make speeches through 1871. She had spoken for the National Women's Suffrage Association, but on November 20, 1871, she spoke at Steinway Hall "to an audience of 3,000 people, to which hundreds found it impossible to obtain admission; which, in consideration of the drenching rain of the evening, is the best evidence of what subject lies nearest the hearts of the people." Her speech stated:

> *Our government is based upon the proposition that: All men and women are born free and equal and entitled to certain inalienable rights, among which are life, liberty and the pursuit of happiness. Now what we, who demand social freedom, ask, is simply that the government of this country shall be administered in accordance with the spirit of this proposition. Nothing more, nothing less.*
>
> *If that proposition means anything, it means just what it says, without qualification, limitation or equivocation. It means that every person who*

Cell at Occoquan Workhouse, Virginia, 1917. These are similar to the conditions women endured when arrested for attempting to vote. *Records of the National Woman's Party, Library of Congress.*

> *comes into the world of outward existence is of equal right as an individual, and is free as an individual, and that he or she is entitled to pursue happiness in whatever direction he or she may choose. Now this is absolutely true of all men and all women. But just here the wise-acres stop and tell us that everybody must not pursue happiness in his or her own way; since to do so absolutely, would be to have no protection against the action of individuals. These good and well-meaning people only see one-half of what is involved in the proposition. They look at a single individual and for the time lose sight of all others. They do not take into their consideration that every other individual beside the one whom they contemplate is equally with him entitled to the same freedom; …*
>
> *To all such persons we assert: that it is freedom and not despotism which we advocate and demand; and we will as rigorously demand that individuals be restricted to their freedom as any person dare to demand; and as rigorously demand that people who are predisposed to be tyrants instead of free men or women shall, by the government, be so restrained as to make the exercise of their proclivities impossible.*[63]

However, the influence of Woodhull was a factor in the deterioration for a time in the relationship between Anthony and Stanton. Many of the suffrage activists and antislavery activists fought for the same causes. However, the slavery issue created a turning point for a large faction of suffragists who did not want to see the issues of suffrage and temperance fought concurrently with the fight for black men's rights. Some of the most vocal dissenters backed Anthony, who was vehemently against temperance being linked with suffrage. Stanton, meanwhile, rallied against the separation of religion from government.

In a speech in January 1871 called "Suffrage and the Working Woman," Anthony voiced her frustration with black men having the vote before women. She used the example of black men as an equivalent to the lot of women:

> *You say the women and the negro are not parallel cases. The negro was a down trodden race, but for the women there is no such necessity for they are lovely and beloved, and the men will guard them from evil. I suppose they will guard their own wives and daughters and mothers and sisters, but is every man as careful to guard another man's wife, daughter, mother, and sister? It is not a question of safety to women in general. It is simply "Is she my property?" ...You women who have kind brothers and husband and sons, I ask you to join with us in this movement so that woman can protect herself.*[64]

By later in the year, matters would change. The time out west would bring Anthony much traction in her movement and followers who would back her financially and provide a space for the cohort of women who were learning how to fight for their rights. Women were getting the right to vote in some states, and Oregon and Washington were Anthony's next targets. Happily, the trip with Abigail coincided with these goals.

Anna Howard Shaw, shown on the following page and discussed briefly elsewhere in this text, was a later figure who loomed large in the suffrage movement. Also pictured is lawyer and reformer Inez Mullholland, who would gain fame in women's rights campaigns and in marching in parades, particularly the March 3, 1913 women's suffrage parade in Washington, D.C., wearing a sweeping white dress atop her horse Grey Dawn. These societies of women were enmeshed and supported one another as frequently as they were able. As societies went, strife and nitpicking could happen, as with Shaw or Woodhull.

Sojourner Truth suffrage card. *Library of Congress.*

Late-period suffragists, in a page from the Miller NAWSA Suffrage Scrapbooks. Lucy Anthony (niece of Susan) and Inez Mulholland (suffragist, labor lawyer and public speaker) can be seen here. *Library of Congress.*

Sojourner Truth spent her life fighting for her own rights and those of other women of color. She initiated sit-ins in horse carriages, where she refused to go back to the segregated cars. "I want to ride," Truth was heard to shout in one such incident. She associated with other protestors who were part of the abolitionist circles of acquaintances in the East.[65]

Chapter 7
The Tour

Any fool can make a quilt; and, after we had made a couple of dozen over twenty years ago, we quit the business with a conviction that nobody but a fool would spend so much time in cutting bits of dry goods into yet small bits and sewing them together again, just for the sake of making believe that they were busy at practical work.

—Abigail Scott Duniway[66]

The start of Anthony's journey north was not under good circumstances. It must have been hard to leave her mentor, Elizabeth Cady Stanton, and yet exciting. She wrote in her diary an account of the boat trip and spared few words. In her book *The Life and Work of Susan B. Anthony*, Ida B. Husted printed the diary excerpt, which she called "near illegible":

> *1st day.—I feel forlorn enough thus left alone on the ocean but I am in for it and bound to go through….Before 6 o'clock my time came and old ocean received my contribution.*
> *2nd day.—Strong gale and rough sea. Tried to dress—no use—back to my berth and there I lay all day. Everybody groaning, babies crying, mothers scolding, the men making quite as much fuss as the women.*
> *3rd day.— Tried to get up but in vain. In the afternoon staggered up on deck—men stretched out on all sides looking as wretched as I felt—glad to get back to bed. Captain sent some frizzled ham and hard tack, with his compliments. Sea growing heavier all the time.*[67]

The trip took in all seven agonizing days, though her journal indicated the weather was calmer toward the end of the trip. Her last boat entry shows her somewhat more cheerful and able to go out on deck. She even discussed the "women question" with some of the passengers in a spirited way before arriving in Portland at ten o'clock in the evening on August 31, 1871, none too soon from her perspective, to meet a "pleasant-faced" Abigail the next day.

She had several days to, as she put it, "get my head straightened" before she was to lecture. The profit of the one to two months of lectures was earmarked to pay off her debt. She had contracted for half of gross receipts for evening lectures and all the receipts from the afternoon ones. The opportunity to speak as top billing rather than second place to Stanton appealed to Anthony as well. It gives one an insight into how she felt, rather than the legend or remote figure we know by the way of her being an esteemed historical figure. She wrote in a letter to her home that she felt that way, saying:

> *I miss Mrs. Stanton, still I can not but enjoy the feeling that people call on* me, *and the fact that I am able to sharpen my wits a little by answering questions and doing the chatting, instead of merely sitting a lay figure and listening to the brilliant scintillations as they emanate from her never-exhausted magazine. There is no alternative—whoever goes into a parlor or before an audience with that woman does it at the cost of a fearful overshadowing, a price which I have paid for the last ten years, and that cheerfully, because I felt that our cause was most profited by her being seen and heard, and my best work was making the way clear for her.*

At first, it was difficult to find places for the women to speak. They were consigned to schoolhouses or theaters when the churches were closed to them. Anthony's first speech in Portland was a somewhat modified version of the one she had done before leaving San Francisco sometime before. Though she showed trepidation at speaking after feeling rejected in California, it was well received. Abigail Scott Duniway, not one to let the occasion go unrecorded, nor to let a good sentence go without a great many parts and commas, said in her autobiography of the first speech:

> *How vividly I recall my first experience before a Portland audience! No Church was open to us anywhere, and the old Orofino Theatre was our only refuge. I went in fear and trembling before a cold, curious and critical*

> *crowd, half bent with weariness resulting from long, continuous mental and physical overwork, and said in a faltering voice, "The movement that arose in the East nearly twenty years ago, to demand Equal Rights for Women, and appeared, at first, a shadow not longer than a woman's hand, has grown and spread from the Atlantic Coast, till it pauses tonight in farthest Oregon, nearly in hearing of the Pacific Ocean. Keeping ahead of that shadow is the illustrious visitor, who illuminates it wherever she goes with the freedom spirit of her devotion. This distinguished visitor is my world-renowned coadjutor, Susan B. Anthony of Everywhere, who will now address you."*[68]

The two women were such passionate speakers about the cause dear to them that they were quickly successful. In some places, they were more what one would call infamous. At times, trash and rotted fruit were thrown at the two women, targets as they were.

Other Portland lectures went well, Anthony and Abigail reported in their journals. *The Oregonian* said, "The audience, which listened attentively and with evident deep interest to this address, was large and chiefly composed of the intelligent portion of our citizens." However, the Portland press was not as kind. The Portland newspaper the *Oregon Herald* published derogatory poetry about the pair. It portrayed the suffragist as "manly" and as a shrill, screeching woman who shook a bony fist at men and, by implication, traditional gender roles of child and home care while she went off to make a living as a congressman. The *Herald* printed this poem under a column:

> *We trust our readers will not miss the perusal of this piece of rhythmical irony. It is certainly one of the happiest hits we have seen for many a day. No one can mistake the allusion to the "Old Gal" who has been so recently among us "tooting her horn."*
> *Along the city's thoroughfare,*
> *A grim Old Gal with manly air*
> *Strode amongst the noisy crowd*
> *Tooting her horn both shrill and loud;*
> *Till e'en over the city's roar*
> *Above its din and discord, o'er*
> *All, was heard, "Ye tyrants, fear*
> *The dawn of freedom's drawing near—*
> *Women's Rights and Suffrage."*[69]

The pair had justifiable success in most places they visited. Newspapers reported crowds at most locations, and the press increased visibility to the cause. Anthony wrote frequently back to her compatriots in the East, as well as to her former newspaper. Abigail wrote that the *New Northwest* "gave Miss Anthony many whole pages of free advertisement for many weeks." The thirty-five-day trip went from Portland for three days, to Salem, northwest to Oregon City, Milwaukie and then back to Portland. Then they sailed on the Columbia River up to the Dalles, Umatilla, Wallula and Walla Walla. South to Albany and Corvallis was next, and then northwest again to Monmouth, Dayton, Lafayette, McMinnville and Forest Grove.

In a letter Abigail wrote to Stanton as they were traveling on the boat up the Columbia River, she tells Stanton that Anthony "has conquered the press and brought the whole fraternity to terms," that "we find the people everywhere enthusiastic and delighted" and that "her fund of logic, fact, and fun seems inexhaustible."[70]

The women visited Abigail's father, John Tucker Scott, for three days as well. Means of travel varied. The tour was made by steamer, on a train, by wagon and on horseback. None of these was particularly comfortable, except perhaps the train, but there are no further reports of sickness on the part of Anthony.

While en route to Wallula, the party stopped for the night in Umatilla. Anthony and Abigail went walking on the shoreline of Umatilla Landing. At the corner store, they came upon a man sitting in front of the building. Anthony was astonished to find that he was the same person who, when he was young, had run away from home in her own neighborhood, and the family thought him long dead. She convinced him to let her write to his mother. His condition was that she share a glass of wine with him. Although she was completely against drinking and known as a staunch teetotaler, she consented to one mouthful of the glass of wine, after which she handed him back the drink. It was unfortunate that she did. Somehow, word reached the Associated Press, which sent out a far-reaching news bulletin that she was behaving improperly. The news would color churchgoers' ideas against her even more.

The variety of venues they spoke at was colorful almost to the point of absurdity, including schools, stores, private residences and even pool halls. The rumors continued, but they made good press. The common theme when they spoke was women's suffrage, but the speeches appealed to reason and common sense as well. Anthony was quoted often as saying, "Married women are no more or less than slaves." Newspapers' accounts said the women's suffrage principles could cause revolution, destruction of homes and general "chaos." Duniway biography *Ladies Were Not Expected* by Dorothy Nafus Morrison quoted one newspaper as saying Anthony's work "would 'destroy all that is pure and beautiful in human nature.'"

A circus-like atmosphere was lent to their talks by the intrusion of a woman who saw Susan B. Anthony as more or less her nemesis and made it her goal to undermine the mission. Mrs. J. Blakesley Frost shadowed their trip and apparently came all the way from her home to mount an "anti-suffrage" campaign of her own. She proceeded to hold rallies and talks in the same towns at similar times to compete for attention and audience; however, her audiences were "much smaller," as the *New Northwest* reported.[71]

Curiously, although Abigail reported on Frost, there isn't much mention of her in many books by and about Susan B. Anthony. Abigail said that in one speech at the Oregon State Fair, Anthony had over one thousand people come to listen to her. At her "rival" speech, Frost drew a crowd of forty, even though she was reported to have "gone for the scalp" of Miss Anthony[72] in a strikingly sexist comment reminiscent of a "catfight." Her opponent's responses spoke to both of their personalities. Anthony and Abigail both saw obstacles as things they could overcome with effort, charm and hard work.

A four-panel cartoon depicting four stages in a man's life. As a child, he laughs at the idea "that women had a right to vote"; later, as a college student, he "denounced Susan B. Anthony"; then, "as a married man he reviled the suffrage movement" to his wife and daughters; and finally, "when suffrage became imminent," he hopped onto the "Votes for Women Band Wagon" and claimed that "we have lived to see reason triumph over prejudice." *John T. McCutcheon,* Puck *magazine, Library of Congress.*

Susan B. Anthony, *seated*, reading a book. *Library of Congress.*

Frost seemed to have been personally affronted by their crusade, while the appearance is that Anthony let the antics of Frost roll right by her without notice and Abigail rather gloated about crowd size in her account. It also speaks to the caricatures of Anthony as aloof, standoffish and remote, while Abigail had a reputation as fiery and given a bit to grandstanding.

The early part of their trip was a capital success, to Abigail at least, in persuading women. "Miss Anthony made scores of converts, and frightened the few old fogies in the city almost out of their wits," she said of Walla Walla in an issue of her paper on October 20, 1871. "The *New Northwest* gained an abundance of new subscribers, and the women are unanimously resolved to use their right to vote."[73] She was as determined and shrewd a businesswoman as ever.

Not all was positive. The Umatilla newspaper felt otherwise and said the woman's vote crusade was "worse than the small-pox and chills and fever combined."[74] And according to a September 17, 1871 *Oregon Statesman* report on Anthony's speech at the Reed Opera House:

> *People may have expected that a champion of the new movement would be something of a scold, but the tones in which she did her scolding—for she scold*[ed] *all of mankind at a terrible rate—were decorous and womanly, so much so that the effect of her lectures was greatly enhanced by the admirable manner and apparent good taste of their delivery.*
>
> ...*We believe that when the first effect of her appearance wears away the women of Oregon will realize that while she told many truths and told them well, she treated their own husbands and fathers unfairly.*[75]

But oh, the fair! The Oregon State Fair was to be a memorable experience for both Susan B. Anthony and Abigail Scott Duniway.

CHAPTER 8

THE FAIR

I do not demand equal pay for any women save those who do equal work in value. Scorn to be coddled by your employers; make them understand that you are in their service as workers, not as women.
—Susan B. Anthony

Abigail waxed eloquently about the fair in the *New Northwest* in later years. She was a woman of travel from her pioneer days, and the hustle agreed with her, as she wrote in "Editorial Correspondence." The picture she created was that of a fair both quaint and modern, a place that truly showcased the best Oregon had to offer along with new and foreign delights:

> *The canvas city, swarming with life and bright with the ruddy glow of a thousand camp-fires, whose ruddy glow painted many a motley group with the extremes of brilliant light and softly swaying shadow, nestling in grotesque irregularity among the dwarf oaks of the fair grounds, presented a suggestive picture, as the train which bore us from the metropolis, heralded by the shrill scream of the engine and loudly proclaiming its near approach by the warning tones of its bell, stopped at the fair grounds on Tuesday evening and discharged its eager mass of living freight....*
>
> *Blatant showmen on every hand made the evening air hideous with noisy proclamation of the wonders that were hidden from the gaze by dingy domes of canvas, the magic portals of which the curious were allowed to*

Satirical cartoon, *Harper's Weekly*, 1907. *Library of Congress.*

pass upon presenting credentials labeled "fifty cents." The usual number of booths, candy stands, cheap John stores, soda fountains, mammoth swings, etc., etc., drew the attention and dimes of the multitude; the circus tent occupied huge space within the enclosure, while outside, near the south gate, Brother Hammond's revival songs rose from beneath the white wings of the "Gospel Tent," and stole softly and sweetly out upon the air of evening.

> *Large letters of gorgeous hue announced that "Reed's Panorama," was again on exhibition; and, by the way, this is the third successive year that this magnificent display of Oregon scenery on canvas has drawn large and admiring audiences at the State Fair.*[76]

The frank racism in this article went unchecked, which was, again, commonplace. The focus on race was a divisive issue for suffrage in many ways and worth many excellent entire books on the subject; for a fascinating treatment, read the article "The Root: How Racism Tainted Women's Suffrage," by Monee Fields-White, on National Public Radio online.[77] It is undeniable that "suffrage" can be viewed in one way as the "white woman's search for rights," and the idea rightfully brings questions to the validity of work that was just as exclusive as traditional male chauvinism and gender prejudice. It was not unusual, especially for the period, but it is disconcerting to see how, in an attempt to show "fair" treatment for women, the bias against race was supremely obvious. It was very much a "one-or-the-other" issue for many prominent activists, Anthony, Duniway and Frederick Douglass included.

The *New Northwest* editorial article by Duniway continued to show an authentic scene from the fair:

> *The arrangement of the Clackamas County fruits displayed exquisite taste and was performed mainly by Mrs. McCue, a well-known resident of Oregon City. Conspicuous above the fruit was a placard announcing that "the work was done exclusively by white labor, employing sixty women and girls." Interrogating the gentlemanly superintendent, Mr. Frank Pyle, (who patiently answered the dozens of questions that were propounded by as many individuals in the space of a few minutes), as to whether this class of operatives were employed in place of men or boys because they could be hired at lower rates, he replied that they were paid according to the labor performed, that work that other establishments were paying Chinamen 90 cents per day for performing, they paid $1.20 a day.*

Susan B. Anthony had much more matter-of-fact things to report in her diary for the first day of the state fair:

> *Up at 5:15—breakfast—and off at 7 a.m.—pressing crowd of people and tents—everybody from all parts of the state come and camp whole week—Afoot is Ryland's Circus Tent—at least 100 people—but less in*

> *ours—got 18 suffragists & dollars for testament committee—Mrs. D. had as many testimonies—I slept in the D's tent tonight—first time in life—Mr. D—Mr. Kelly—3 boys—Clara—Mrs. D—& self, packed side by side like herrings—can't say I liked it better than nice bedroom & hair mattress.*[78]

Abigail, in contrast, was happy to share her family's camp with Anthony. She called the camp "a cozy little shanty, renovated each year by carpets and beds of fresh, cleanest straw, and affording a delightful little nook wherein to rest and dress and sleep."[79] As a happy traveler, in general, she was a child of the West, albeit an imported one, and her affinity for the land and the outdoors was a departure from Anthony's outlook. Either way, the fair was one both would recall long afterward.

In her autobiography, Abigail would write:

> *When the annual State Fair of Oregon convened at Salem, Miss Anthony camped with my family on the grounds, her first experience of camping out. There was no assembly hall at that time on the Fair Grounds, and we held an open-air meeting in the shade of the pavilion, where the shrieking of whistles and the blare of drums and brass-instruments, combined with the spieling of side-show promoters, compelled us to speak with a screeching accent, but brought us much commendation from a large and intelligent audience, and secured us many subscriptions to* The New Northwest.[80]

Contrast that with Anthony's takeaway, when she wrote about "sleeping like herrings" and seemed to prefer not to camp outdoors again.

After "eating dirt, breathing smoke, and sleeping on the ground," they were off to Olympia, Washington. The trip there was another unforgettable escapade. The near-one-hundred-mile drive in a wagon was over corduroy road, which was a commonly used term for a dirt road, strengthened in muddy or swampy areas by logs placed perpendicular to it. The mud would have sucked the hooves of the horses and kept them mired in muck in the worst spots. Even for women accustomed to travel, the Northwest weather was dreadful and the accommodations adequate at best. "It has rained part of every twenty-four hours since we reached Olympia," Anthony lamented when she wrote home.

The Olympia crowd was not as receptive nor as large. Part of the proceeds of one evening were promised to those who were hurt in the Chicago Fire, which Anthony augmented with money of her own, as she felt it made a poor showing. Abigail wrote that in Olympia, Anthony "was on hand with her invincible army of facts about the Power of the Ballot." She also said that of the people who listened—for an hour and forty minutes, no less—"all were converted except an obtuse Johnny Bull, whom we'll gather into our fold at the Women Suffrage convention on the 8th of November."[81]

Tired and rundown, the women rallied their spirits and then made their way through smaller towns that mainly ignored their message. In one instance, the women were invited to a private home by a woman who had attended a lecture, and they went home with her. When her husband arrived home, startled, he tossed the lecturers out, saying he did not run a hotel. Abigail wished to argue their case. Anthony prevailed, and they withdrew back to public lodging instead.

The crown accomplishment of the trip was an invitation to speak at the Washington territorial legislature. On October 18, Anthony was invited to dinner with Judge Daniel R. Bigelow and his wife, Ann Elizabeth White Bigelow. Bigelow was a Washington politician and women's rights activist. He and his wife, who had come from the East Coast originally, had been active in politics and antislavery efforts there in the same suffragist circles. Bigelow had a completely different manner by which he thought women could vote.

Bigelow had brought a suffrage bill a few days earlier to the Washington territorial legislature concerning women's rights. His bill would "authorize women on whether or not they wanted to vote," according to a paper by researcher Shanna Stevenson.[82] In other words, he wanted to take the temperature to see if enough women wanted to vote at all before they got the right to do so. Anthony was justifiably opposed to this idea. When the legislature voted on October 17 on whether to have Anthony come speak for her cause, the motion passed, eighteen votes to eight.[83]

The Washington territorial legislature address is considered one of Anthony's better speeches. The trusty *New Northwest* didn't let the opportunity go by and printed the retelling of the speech near a column of Abigail's "editorial Correspondences," detailing the trip.

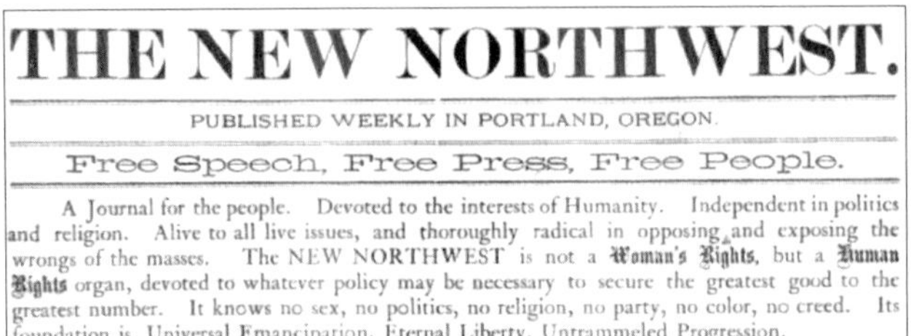
THE NEW NORTHWEST.

PUBLISHED WEEKLY IN PORTLAND, OREGON.

Free Speech, Free Press, Free People.

A Journal for the people. Devoted to the interests of Humanity. Independent in politics and religion. Alive to all live issues, and thoroughly radical in opposing and exposing the wrongs of the masses. The NEW NORTHWEST is not a Woman's Rights, but a Human Rights organ, devoted to whatever policy may be necessary to secure the greatest good to the greatest number. It knows no sex, no politics, no religion, no party, no color, no creed. Its foundation is, Universal Emancipation, Eternal Liberty, Untrammeled Progression.

The *New Northwest* masthead. *Oregon Digital Newspaper Program.*

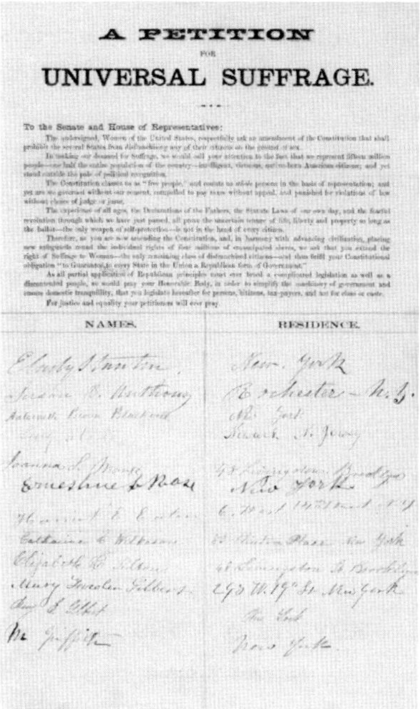

A PETITION

FOR

UNIVERSAL SUFFRAGE.

To the Senate and House of Representatives:

For justice and equality your petitioners will ever pray.

NAMES. RESIDENCE.

Petition from Susan B. Anthony and Elizabeth Cady Stanton to the United States Senate, circa December 1874. *U.S. National Archives.*

In the speech, for which Anthony was wearing a gray silk gown that she had remarked on wearing in a previous talk, she said, "The theory of our government is embodied by the Declaration of Independence which declares that 'all men are created equal: that we are endowed by our Creator with certain unaliable [*sic*] rights.'" Her speech continued in the same measured vein, calmly enumerating the reasonable assertions she as a woman had for believing they had the same rights as any man. One of her main points—that the Constitution applied to all people, not just men—was argued against by some members of the legislature by the use of male pronouns. If that was so, she argued, then the other laws, such as those concerning taxation, should only apply to men also.

Abigail concluded her report on the speech with: "She warned those having political aspirations that now was the accepted time of salvation: to take heed of the indications of the times, before it was too late. Already many men were filled with fear and trembling, and she urged them to hesitate no longer and embrace the inevitable logic of events."

Anthony wrote succinctly: "October 19 Thursday. Olympia Wash Ter Addressed Legislature at 2 P.M. Assembly room packed—Made pretty good argument."

The speech had good reviews in some quarters. The appearance spurred Anthony and Abigail to help others form the Washington Women's Suffrage Association. The lobbying by this group, Anthony and Abigail Scott Duniway put so much pressure on the Washington legislature that the men of that body passed an 1871 law making it illegal for women to vote until women could legally vote in the entire United States. Many bills gave and then revoked women's suffrage between 1871 and 1906 in the territory. Oddest of these was an incident in 1897, when a false bill was substituted for a constitutionally amending bill to allow suffrage during a recess; reform worker Laura Hall Peters found it and made sure it was signed by Governor John Rogers, but the bill ultimately failed. The groups that Anthony and Abigail helped form did persist, and eventually Washington voted to allow women's suffrage in 1910.[84]

Chapter 9

Division

Women, we might as well be dogs baying the moon as petitioners without the right to vote!
—Susan B. Anthony[85]

The trip ended with Anthony's last talk not as successful as she would have liked. Talks in Olympia brought serenades and marriage proposals. Portland, and the rainy season, brought with it melancholy. In fact, she wrote it was like "mortal agony" and on her trip home lamented that she was "as single-handed and penniless as usual."

Her diary from November 15 said: "Terrible depression of spirit with feeling of impossibility to mark this last speech in Portland....Altogether, it was the most terrible, oppressive of my life of trying."[86]

Some of her down spirit could have been from the incessant bad weather, no doubt. It was not the only off note in the trip, but overall the journey had opened minds and brought the word of suffrage to thousands of people who might not otherwise have experienced it. On her way down the coast to California, Anthony continued to lecture and kept Abigail informed by writing her letters along the way. "I particularly recall her favorable mention of Dr. Bethenia Owens, of Roseburg (now Dr. Owens-Adair), who arranged a successful meeting for her at the Douglas County Court House and entertained her in her home," Abigail wrote.

Anthony continued her journey to equal suffrage in California and elsewhere, drawing support from old friends. Despite Anthony's warnings

Susan B. Anthony. By Frances Benjamin Johnston, *The World's Work*, 1906. *Wikipedia*.

to always speak from meticulously prepared notes and not to spout unprepared arguments, Abigail gave extemporaneous speeches in support of her cause often. Her style was flavored with her own history and used vivid images and vignettes in both her written word and personal appearances. Her popularity drew from her appeal to the woman of the West who was awakening to the idea that there was more to life for herself than chores, and her novels and newspaper articles only added to that. Her wry sense of humor certainly shows, and it was this kind of story that was repeated by Abigail as she campaigned. She almost became a character in one of her own stories. She was larger than life. Her argument, much like Susan B. Anthony's, tried to get to a common ground between men and women and point out the inequities. The manner was effective. The folk stories she related in the speeches were what took hold and were remembered.

One such story was related in her autobiography. She was lecturing on her own, enjoying the time and publicity shortly after Anthony left. At one stop in Gervais, she was told a new male lawyer wanted to argue points with her, but she had been hired for a lecture, not a debate; despite her willingness to debate for the first time on her own, it was voted down at the meeting. She lectured. At the end, Abigail mentioned, "I didn't want to be dispensing any false doctrines," and said that if any of the women felt that she had "poisoned the minds of any of the young ladies in the 'Amen Corner,'" she wanted them to summon the lawyer and they would debate after all.

The crowd went wild. The young man argued with humorous quips and generally said that if women got to vote they "would desert their homes for lawyers' offices and judges' seats, leaving the deserted men to quiet the babies the best they could, with rubber substitutes." His backward apology consisted of explaining away his crudeness because

British suffrage poster: "Read our paper. Votes for women," 1920. *Schlesinger Library at Harvard University.*

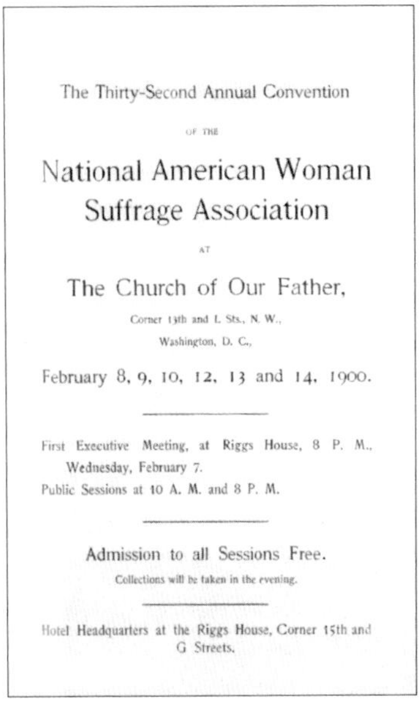
The Thirty-Second Annual Convention

OF THE

National American Woman Suffrage Association

AT

The Church of Our Father,

Corner 13th and L Sts., N. W.,

Washington, D. C.,

February 8, 9, 10, 12, 13 and 14, 1900.

First Executive Meeting, at Riggs House, 8 P. M., Wednesday, February 7.

Public Sessions at 10 A. M. and 8 P. M.

Admission to all Sessions Free.

Collections will be taken in the evening.

Hotel Headquarters at the Riggs House, Corner 15th and G Streets.

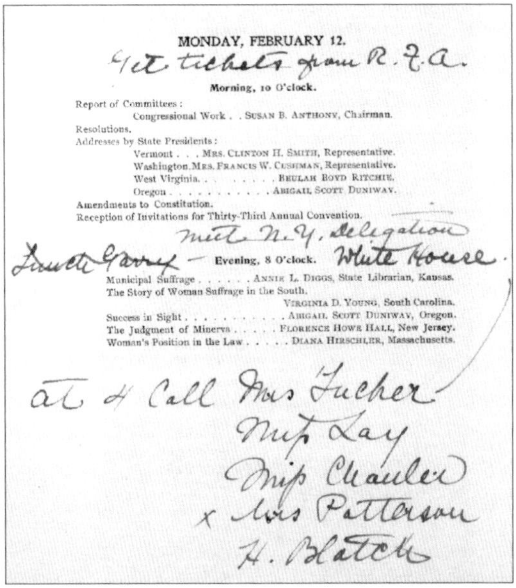
MONDAY, FEBRUARY 12.

Morning, 10 O'clock.

Report of Committees:
Congressional Work . . SUSAN B. ANTHONY, Chairman.
Resolutions.
Addresses by State Presidents:
Vermont . . . MRS. CLINTON H. SMITH, Representative.
Washington. MRS. FRANCIS W. CUSHMAN, Representative.
West Virginia. . . . . BEULAH BOYD RITCHIE.
Oregon . . . . ABIGAIL SCOTT DUNIWAY.
Amendments to Constitution.
Reception of Invitations for Thirty-Third Annual Convention.

Evening, 8 O'clock.

Municipal Suffrage . . . . . . ANNIE L. DIGGS, State Librarian, Kansas.
The Story of Woman Suffrage in the South.
VIRGINIA D. YOUNG, South Carolina.
Success in Sight . . . . ABIGAIL SCOTT DUNIWAY, Oregon.
The Judgment of Minerva . . . . . FLORENCE HOWE HALL, New Jersey.
Woman's Position in the Law . . . . . DIANA HIRSCHLER, Massachusetts.

Left: Thirty-Second National American Women's Suffrage Association convention program, 1900. *Library of Congress.*

Right: Thirty-Second National American Women's Suffrage Association convention program, showing Susan B. Anthony and Abigail Scott Duniway speaking in the morning session, 1900. *Library of Congress.*

he was a manual laborer, not at all like Abigail. His parting blow was a joke about how he'd often heard a hen try to crow but had not seen one accomplish it yet.

She destroyed him. Sweetly, she said that she hadn't needed the confirmation from the moderator about the lawyer being single. She hoped one of the ladies there would "someday be kind enough to initiate him into the mysteries of matrimony and maternity and cure him of his present agony of fear" that if women were enfranchised they would neglect their children or there would be no more children. To his manual labor comment, she retorted that apparently, he didn't know much about physical work, because she herself had "milked enough milk with my own two hands" to make the biggest steamboat in the area at the time float. She had "made butter enough for market with the propelling power of my hands at an old-fashioned churn, during nine previous years of my life on a farm, to grease the axles of creation." His last point she conceded, having often seen hens try to crow without success. But, she finished to wild enthusiasm, "I once saw a rooster try to set, and he made a failure too."[87]

Her efforts were part of what she called a "still hunt" campaign: to work for equality by lecturing and proselytizing to persuade influential voters to give women their rights. It was kind of a behind-the-scenes industry. She worked to set up suffrage societies where she spoke so that women could establish centers for the women there to work on their own. The curious dichotomy of campaigning for women while trying to appeal to men she put this way:

> *I kept up my journeying with almost continuous regularity, carrying the gospel of equal rights into all parts of Oregon, Washington, and Idaho, making converts everywhere, especially among the men, whom I could more*

Left: A caricature showing "Political boss" conducting a chorus, with woman "anti" in front of men "procurer," "dive-keeper," "child labor employer," "grafter," "cadet" and "sweat shop owner." *Library of Congress.*

Right: A postcard showing a girl holding up her finger to a boy and this poem: "For the work of a day, for the taxes we pay, for the laws we obey, we want something to say," 1913. *Library of Congress.*

easily reach in their stores and offices than their wives in their homes and kitchens, never forgetting that one convert with a vote was worth a hundred who possessed the secondary and almost negligible power of "influence."

Eventually, she became disillusioned with the organization of societies for suffrage and spent her time with more writing, canvassing for subscribers and lectures. Her efforts were recorded in the *New Northwest* and the other varied papers she wrote for, including Anthony's newspaper. In the 1872 presidential election, she and three other women attempted to vote. This endeavor was echoed by other suffragists across the nation, notably Susan B. Anthony. In Oregon, Abigail Scott Duniway, Mrs. M.A. Lambert, Mrs. Beatty and Maria Hendee tried to vote. Beatty was an African American woman who, along with Hendee, had worked with Duniway in the Oregon State Equal Suffrage Association. Their votes did not actually get counted—they were stuck under the ballot box by a judge—but what they did associated their action on the West Coast with the activists on the East Coast.[88] The timing lent an air of legitimacy and continuity to the suffrage movement, even if it did not grant them the vote at that time.

As time went by, Abigail's style increasingly came into conflict with others' ideas for how the process should work. She was vehemently opposed to linking the suffrage cause with those who supported temperance. She was not opposed to the idea of temperance and had been a charter member of the Temperance Alliance in Oregon when it was founded. She had even written much of the constitution of the organization. Her fear was that the economic element, specifically the liquor manufacturers, would overwhelm the suffrage issue.

Her qualm was that "every attempt of men to prohibit economic rights for women has ever since increased my feeling of opposition to any sort of prohibition which would destroy the moral responsibility or right to self-control in any man or woman." She was actively against the Woman's Christian Temperance Union and its many followers in the late 1870s to 1880s "because it diverted female organizational energy from women's rights, antagonized too many voters, and mobilized the powerful opposition of the liquor interests," according to historian Rebecca J. Mead in her book *How the Vote Was Won: Women Suffrage in the United States, 1868–1914*.[89] In 1879, she was met with what was called "Jacksonville Arguments," a barrage of eggs thrown at her by what were purported to be the leading men of Jacksonville, a mining town in southern Oregon, when she attempted to speak there.

"A female suffrage fancy." Joseph Keppler, 1880. Composite of eight caricatures showing women dressing and interacting in society as men; drinking; voting for handsome candidates; driving ugly men from the polls; and a domestic scene showing a man taking care of children. *Library of Congress.*

Two years previously, her controversial methods and stubborn attitude had caused other leaders of the Oregon State Equal Suffrage Association to ask Abigail to step down as the leader of the organization. Two female physician members, Dr. Mary A. Thompson and Dr. Bethenia Owens-Adair, urged her to leave, saying she stood in the way of success of the movement.

She left to travel through Idaho, where her family was attempting to settle once again. Touring and lecturing through that state and Washington off and on for about ten years gave her widespread influence. Her children and sisters, and their children, established in locations dispersed around the Northwest and were good emissaries for her work; many of them started suffrage associations of their own and brought the newspaper she owned to their locales. Abigail spent time writing fiction, too. The *New Northwest* published an article written by Abigail claiming that the purpose of her writing was to "lay the facts before you; facts as parables; facts as lessons; facts as they are in the every-day life of more than one woman who pursues the allotted rounds of a life of heroic effort." The paper was bought in 1886. In short succession, Wilkie, Hubert and Willis Duniway settled themselves as businessmen, with Harvey Scott's assistance.[90]

Abigail came back to a suffrage association where, in her words, "not a single meeting had been called, and no steps of any kind had been taken for advancing the movement; so I was compelled to begin where I had left off, after the defeat of a previous decade." It was not an easy time. Granted, this was rather par for the course where Abigail was concerned. The foes made by her actions had not forgotten their enmity. The newer women's rights association gave the old records "to a new administration created to sidetrack my work," Abigail wrote, "and were never heard of afterwords [*sic*]."

Much has been made of the cantankerous professional relationships that Abigail had, and chose not to have, with others in the suffrage movement. Some of the strife seems to have been from jealousy, but some is due to her strident manner and firm beliefs, no doubt. Despite her personal relationship with Anthony, their friendship was abruptly changed in 1889 after the National Woman Suffrage Association (NWSA) convention. Speaking against the prohibition, Abigail drew a final line through which they did not come unscathed. Her speech against prohibition contained things like

> *Too many men and women are making money, notoriety, travel and fame, as its proponents, to expect it to be abandoned without a prolonged and excited struggle. Too many cases of the abuse of the traffic, by men and women who have made the sale of intoxicants their business but have failed to deal honestly in controlling and exploiting the traffic, and too many cases of cruelty, crime and poverty have been traced to the saloon, to expect this conflict to cease until the saloon shall have reformed itself.*

And

> *On the other hand, too many men depend on the production, transportation, and sale of wheat, barley, hops, rye, apples, peaches, berries, grapes and cherries, from which intoxicants are made, and too many men are employed in their making and marketing, all of whom depend directly or indirectly on the traffic; too many men are engaged in transporting these commodities from the farms to the breweries, distilleries, and wineries, and thence to the whole sale and retail dealers, and from these to the consumer.*[91]

She extrapolated on through the industry this way in her speech for two pages and cited the impact on the hotel and restaurant trade, the shopkeepers, the private rentals, the canneries, bakeries and blacksmiths and

"Ancient History," *Life* magazine, February 20, 1913. *Library of Congress.*

so on, all the way down to the preacher who must bury a drunk. She ends with: "Let the blame go to the drunkard, where it belongs; let the drunkard's wife have legal power to protect her home from the debauchery, just as the husband has the power, when so inclined, to protect it now." The argument is sound from a modern perspective taken that way, and politically, Abigail and her family were staunch businesspeople. It makes sense without the lean on "morality" of the advertisements of the day, for instance. Those put the woman firmly in the home in shame-based techniques best illustrated by having men perform traditional "female tasks," like cleaning and child care. Ruth Barnes Moynihan called it "a society that expected women to be purer and better than men."[92]

The blowback from this speech, which she used in part for the NWSA convention as well, was immense. Supporters distanced themselves. The Woman's Christian Temperance Union, and its constituents, were outraged, and their support ceased; how could they support suffrage when it detracted from their main goal? Susan B. Anthony distanced herself as well. Abigail called them out and said that those who had spoken against her message—namely suffragists like Elizabeth Cady Stanton, Mary A. Livermore, Susan B. Anthony, Lucretia Mott, Julia Ward Howe, Harriet Beecher Stowe and Lucy Stone—were due thanks "for the help they gave us when they meant to hinder."[93]

Abigail persisted. Driven from her associations, she diverted her work to Idaho, where her family had moved. She continued to work both behind the scenes, in her preferred fashion, and in writing and speeches. Occasionally she demurred and wrote such in her autobiography: "I realize that everybody has a right to a pet hobby, provided, of course, that he doesn't strike down other people's liberties with his hobby horse." But her fight continued through sicknesses and setbacks.

In 1905, the Lewis and Clark Exposition, of which Harvey Scott was coincidentally a board member, honored Abigail by declaring Abigail Scott Duniway Day on October 6. She published a newspaper report on the event in her autobiography: "Mrs. Duniway has been one of the most conspicuous women in the history of the Northwest, and the graceful courtesy of the Exposition officials in recognizing the inestimable value of her services in the development and progress of this state is being heartily commended by the public."

Abigail worked on the campaigns in Oregon of 1900, 1906 and 1908. The effort was enhanced by the return of the National American Woman Suffrage Association (NAWSA) to Portland to help campaign in 1906 and Clara Colby's move to the state to publish her own pro-suffrage paper. She introduced the "Taxpayer's Suffrage Amendment" in 1908 and garnered much more support in Oregon by proposing that every citizen, including women, who pays taxes be given the right to vote. Anna Howard Shaw

Clara Belle Duniway Stearns. Clara, who helped Abigail both in their millinery shop and with the *New Northwest* newspaper, later married Don Stearns. They had one son (Earl) before Clara died of tuberculosis at age thirty-one. Abigail grieved her loss terribly. *Photo by Bob Speckman.*

and Abigail had a personal squabble stemming from Shaw's feeling that Duniway's criticism of prohibition had cost them money and influence in the loss of the 1906 campaign. Support from brother Harvey of *The Oregonian* was withheld until he died in 1910, after which it published pro-suffrage articles.

Women who had been working for suffrage in the state, including Viola Coe, who had at times been president of the women's voting association in Abigail's place, helped mount a campaign for the right to vote and gather signatures for a petition. The general population was much more receptive to the idea, no doubt because they were sandwiched between two states that had already given women the vote: Washington (1910) and California (1911). Meanwhile, Abigail was stricken with pneumonia in February 1912. Later, she contracted blood poisoning and was forced to undergo a two-inch incision sans anesthetic to drain the wound. It took some time for her to recover, but she fought sickness with characteristic tenacity.

One of Abigail's staunchest defenders was Dr. Marie Equi, who was brave enough to stand up to Anna Howard Shaw. A scandal developed within the movement when Shaw attempted to help organize a coup to take over the

Margaret Howe holding an "Oregon" plaque in the suffrage parade in Washington, D.C., 1913. *Records of the Women's Bureau, Record Group 86, U.S. National Archives.*

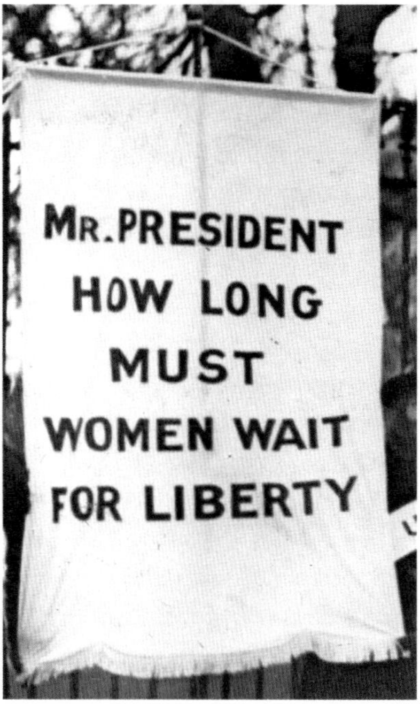

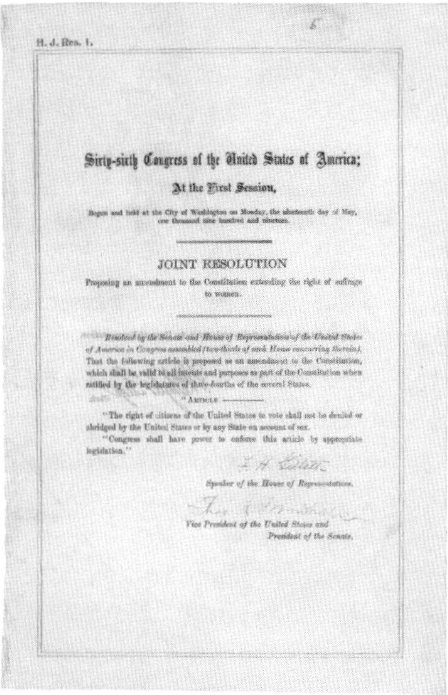

H. J. Res. 1.

Sixty-sixth Congress of the United States of America;

At the First Session,

Begun and held at the City of Washington on Monday, the nineteenth day of May, one thousand nine hundred and nineteen.

JOINT RESOLUTION

Proposing an amendment to the Constitution extending the right of suffrage to women.

Resolved by the Senate and House of Representatives of the United States of America in Congress assembled (two-thirds of each House concurring therein), That the following article is proposed as an amendment to the Constitution, which shall be valid to all intents and purposes as part of the Constitution when ratified by the legislatures of three-fourths of the several States.

"ARTICLE ——

"The right of citizens of the United States to vote shall not be denied or abridged by the United States or by any State on account of sex.

"Congress shall have power to enforce this article by appropriate legislation."

Speaker of the House of Representatives.

Vice President of the United States and President of the Senate.

Above: Women Suffrage fiftieth anniversary stamp. *Smithsonian National Postal Museum; image enlarged, rendered for tone and clarity by Gwillhickers.*

Top, left: A banner from a suffrage parade, 1913. *Library of Congress.*

Top, right: The Nineteenth Amendment. *Library of Congress.*

Oregon State Equal Suffrage Association by donating money anonymously. Equi thought herself neutral up to that point and told Shaw in an incredible fourteen-page letter exactly what she thought of Shaw's attempt to sway things because of her personal feelings about Duniway. Shaw had, according to Equi, tried to overthrow Duniway through innuendo and slander with a woman in the Oregon State Equal Suffrage Association, Sarah Evans:

> *I may yet tell it all, to a yearning reporter, over my signature, and remember, I have witnesses. They must keep hands off Mrs. D in the future, and they must have their instructions to this effect from you; otherwise, I will forget the CAUSE and remember only, there is a woman sick, not only in body but in heart, a woman too old to be wearied and annoyed by heartless woman* [sic] *who are filled with political greed.*[94]

Shortly after Abigail's seventy-eighth birthday party in 1912—attended by Governor West of Oregon, the mayor of Seattle, colonels and an ex-senator—another suffrage vote was taken in Oregon. It passed. Abigail Scott Duniway, who wrote the Women's Emancipation Proclamation for Governor West, was the first registered woman to vote in Multnomah County.

Abigail had been suspicious for some time that she might have diabetes. After having two toes removed, she cared for the wound with her own methods, stubborn as ever, but eventually succumbed. She died in 1915 from an infection on her toe. She did not live to see the passage of the Nineteenth Amendment giving women the right to vote nationwide.

Chapter 10
Susan Succeeds

I distrust those people who know so well what God wants them to do, because I notice it always coincides with their own desires.
—*Susan B. Anthony,* History of Woman Suffrage[95]

Susan B. Anthony was celebrated and reviled for her attempt to vote in the presidential election of 1872. She was arrested along with fifteen others and refused to pay the $500 fine. She was the only one of all the women who were arrested to face trial, and as the leader, her fate would determine whether the right to vote and the action of voting was legal and valid.[96]

Before her trial, she traveled and gave the same lecture in her defense forty-one times. She said, in part:

> *Friends and Fellow-citizens: I stand before you to-night, under indictment for the alleged crime of having voted at the last Presidential election, without having a lawful right to vote. It shall be my work this evening to prove to you that in thus voting, I not only committed no crime, but, instead, simply exercised my citizen's right, guaranteed to me and all United States citizens by the National Constitution, beyond the power of any State to deny.*
>
> *Our democratic-republican government is based on the idea of the natural right of every individual member thereof to a voice and a vote in making and executing the laws....*

A crowd of women registers for jury duty, Portland, Oregon, 1912; Marie Equi is in the front row (hat with bow). *By Gardiner P. Bissel,* Oregon Journal.

"All men are created equal, and endowed by their Creator with certain unalienable rights. Among these are life, liberty and the pursuit of happiness. That to secure these, governments are instituted among men, deriving their just powers from the consent of the governed."

Here is no shadow of government authority over rights, nor exclusion of any from their full and equal enjoyment. Here is pronounced the right of all men, and "consequently," as the Quaker preacher said, "of all women," to a voice in the government. And here, in this very first paragraph of the declaration, is the assertion of the natural right of all to the ballot; for, how can "the consent of the governed" be given, if the right to vote be denied. Again:

"That whenever any form of government becomes destructive of these ends, it is the right of the people to alter or abolish it, and to institute a new government, laying its foundations on such principles, and organizing its powers in such forms as to them shall seem most likely to effect their safety and happiness."

Surely, the right of the whole people to vote is here clearly implied....

The preamble of the federal constitution says:

"We, the people of the United States, in order to form a more perfect union, establish justice, insure domestic tranquility, provide for the common

defense, promote the general welfare and secure the blessings of liberty to ourselves and our posterity, do ordain and establish this constitution for the United States of America."

It was we, the people, not we, the white male citizens, nor yet we, the male citizens; but we, the whole people, who formed this Union. And we formed it, not to give the blessings or liberty, but to secure them; not to the half of ourselves and the half of our posterity, but to the whole people—women as well as men. And it is downright mockery to talk to women of their enjoyment of the blessings of liberty while they are denied the use of the only means of securing them provided by this democratic-republican government—the ballot.[97]

In her trial, she was indicted with this statement:

The defendant is indicted under the 19th section of the Act of Congress of May 31, 1870 (16 St. at L., 144,), for "voting without having a lawful right to vote."...

The only alleged ground of illegality of the defendant's vote is that she is a woman. If the same act had been done by her brother under the same circumstances, the act would have been not only innocent, but honorable and laudable; but having been done by a woman it is said to be a crime.

Speaking in her defense was Judge Henry R. Selden, whom she had consulted on the right to vote:

This is a case of no ordinary magnitude, although many might regard it as one of very little importance. The question whether my client here had done anything to justify her being consigned to a felon's prison or not, is one that interests her very essentially, and that interests the people also essentially. I claim and shall endeavor to establish before you that when she offered to have her name registered as a voter, and when she offered her vote for Member of Congress, she was as much entitled to vote as any man that voted at that election, according to the Constitution and laws of the Government under which she lives. If I maintain that proportion, as a matter of course she has committed no offence, and is entitled to be discharged at your hands.

But, beyond that, whether she was a legal vote or not, whether she was entitled to vote or not, if she sincerely believed that she had a right to vote, and offered her ballot in good faith, under that belief, whether right or wrong, by the laws of this country she is guilty of no crime....

> *I may have been mistaken in that, and if I was mistaken, I believe she acted in good faith. I believe she acted according to her right as the law and Constitution gave it to her. But whether she did or not, she acted in the most perfect good faith, and if she made a mistake, or if I made one, that is not a reason for committing her to a felon's cell.*
>
> *For the second time in my life, in my professional practice, I am under the necessity of offering myself as a witness for my client.*
>
> *Before the last election, Miss Anthony called upon me for advice, upon the question whether she was or was not a legal voter. I examined the question, and gave her my opinion, unhesitatingly, that the laws and Constitution of the United States, authorized her to vote, as well as they authorize any man to vote; and I advised her to have her name placed upon the registry and to vote at the election, if the inspectors should receive her vote. I gave the advice in good faith, believing it to be accurate, and I believe it to be accurate still.*[98]

At the end of the trial segment, the judge read a statement he had prepared. "He said: 'The 14th Amendment gives no right to a woman to vote, and the voting of Miss Anthony was in violation of the law.' Then the judge told the jury to record a guilty verdict without any deliberation. Complaints were made but the ruling stood. She refused to pay and the judge could have made her go to jail. If he had done so, her case could have been taken further—even as far as the Supreme Court—because she had been denied a right to a jury of her peers."[99]

After they parted ways, Susan B. Anthony had distanced herself from Abigail's "still hunt" method of campaigning by persuading influential and wealthy patrons to vote their way. Instead, she espoused the more modern grass-roots method of building teams and collective unions of support. It was akin to the "organic intellectual" concept brought to light by Gramsci's concept of Marxism. In this idea,

> *Traditional intellectuals are those intellectuals linked to tradition and to past intellectuals; those who are not so directly linked to the economic structure of their particular society and, in fact, conceive of themselves as having no basis in any social class and adhering to no particular class discourse or political discourse. Organic intellectuals, on the other hand, are more directly related to the economic structure of their society simply because of the fact that "every social group that originates in the fulfillment of an essential task of economic production" creates its*

> *own organic intellectual. Thus, the organic intellectual "gives his class homogeneity and awareness of its own function, in the economic field and on the social and political levels."*[100]

In practical language, using this method in suffrage terms was to appeal to those who had economic traction within a group. Thus, helping all helped themselves. For instance, in 1877, Anthony campaigned in small mining towns in Colorado with Lucy Stone and Henry Blackwell. There they met in open-air and Latino communities, sometimes with a translator to speak to the crowd in Spanish. They found that a political party's backing would increase their chance of success along with the popular vote. The promotion of voting in outlying areas was the effort that caused the vote to pass; all was thought lost until the rural votes were counted when women's rights finally passed in the state of California.

Anthony's status was such that she was invited to speak at the World's Congress of Representative Women in 1893, where she said:

> *We have known how to make the noise, you see, and how to bring the whole world to our organization in spirit, if not in person. I would philosophize on the reason why. It is because women have been taught always to work for something else than their own personal freedom; and the hardest thing in the world is to organize women for the one purpose of securing their political liberty and political equality. It is easy to congregate thousands and hundreds of thousands of women to try to stay the tide of intemperance; to try to elevate the morals of a community; to try to educate the masses of people; to try to relieve the poverty of the miserable; but it is a very difficult thing to make the masses of women, any more than the masses of men, congregate in great numbers to study the cause of all the ills of which they complain, and to organize for the removal of that cause; to organize for the establishment of great principles that will be sure to bring about the results which they so much desire.*

The World's Congress of Representative Women was part of the Chicago World's Fair of that year. Notable speakers of the day, including Anthony, Julia Ward Howe, Elizabeth Cady Stanton and Ida Husted Harper, attended and lamented the fact that instead of the majority of women needed to persuade the national Congress to change, they numbered about seven thousand. The topic of Anthony's speech was "Organization among Women as an Instrument in Promoting the Interests of Political Liberty." Other speakers had subjects like "Literature and Dramatic Art" and "Science and Religion."[101]

Anthony was incensed when Republican involvement helped the suffrage efforts in Kansas fail in 1894. The Populists were attractive to Anthony because they would support the suffrage ideals. In 1895, she took her speeches to California at the 1895 Women's Congress. The suffrage ideas thrived in San Francisco under leaders like Laura Deforce Gordon. She worked elsewhere for a time and came back to run the state suffrage campaign. They lost, though much traction was made.[102]

In 1895 and 1898, Anthony collaborated with Elizabeth Cady Stanton on a revision of the Bible entitled *The Women's Bible.* In it, writers like Lucy Stone wrote their own interpretation of Bible passages; Stone learned Greek and Latin in order to translate and decode the meaning for herself. It was radical, too radical for the general populace, and by the time the second half of the book came out in 1898, Stanton had been pushed to the side of the suffrage movement. She wasn't asked to sit in the honored spot on stage at the NAWSA convention again.[103]

She kept on lecturing until her large debt was paid off, a move that was applauded by many, though it had taken her ten years. "When she was seventy-four," Arnold Cheney wrote in the book *People of Purpose*, "she was traveling up to one hundred miles a week and speaking five or six nights each week."[104] Anthony undertook a still larger project, the five-volume book *History of Woman Suffrage*, the first part of which was published in 1887. She cowrote it with Elizabeth Cady Stanton, Matilda Joslyn Gage and Ida Husted Harper. In 1900, due to Anthony's persistence, women began to be admitted to the University of Rochester.

Susan B. Anthony, full-length portrait (*seated, facing left*), produced between 1880 and 1906. *Library of Congress.*

Along with Harper, Anthony wrote her life story in *The Life and Work of Susan B. Anthony: A Story of the Evolution of the Status of Women* in 1898. She kept up appearing for as long as she could, single-mindedly working toward her cause with vigor of mind, if not in body at the end. She was able to meet with President Theodore Roosevelt in 1905 to push women's equality and lobbied for suffrage with him in a personal appeal.

On March 13, 1906, Susan B. Anthony died of complications of heart disease and pneumonia. The *New York Times* reported that in a conversation with her friend and co-worker Anna Howard Shaw, she said, "To think I have had more than 60 years of hard struggle for a little liberty, and then to die without it seems so cruel."[105]

She was honored with her likeness on the dollar coin by the United States in 1979.

Appendix A

Works by Abigail Scott Duniway and Susan B. Anthony

Works by Abigail Scott Duniway

Adapted from a list by Debra Shein (Riddle, 2008)

"Amie and Henry Lee, or the Spheres of the Sexes." Serialized in the *New Northwest*, May 29, 1874–November 13, 1874.

"Bijah's Surprises" (revised 1914 as "Margaret Rudson: A Pioneer Story"). Serialized in the *New Northwest*, April 2, 1896–September 26, 1896.

"Blanche Le Clerq: A Tale of the Mountain Mines." Serialized in the *New Northwest*, September 2, 1886–February 24, 1887.

Captain Gray's Company, or Crossing the Plains and Living in Oregon. Portland: S.J. McCormick, 1859. Later serialized in the *New Northwest*, May 21, 1875–October 29, 1875.

"The De Launcy Curse, or The Law of Heredity: A Tale of Three Generations." Serialized in the *New Northwest*, September 10, 1885–March 4, 1886.

"Dux: A Maiden Who Dared." Serialized in the *New Northwest*, September 11, 1884–March 5, 1885.

"Edna and John: A Romance of Idaho Flat." Serialized in the *New Northwest*, September 29, 1875–June 15, 1877.

"Ellen Dowd, the Farmer's Wife." Serialized in the *New Northwest*, part one, January 5, 1872–April 1872.

"Fact, Fate and Fancy, or More Ways of Living than One." Serialized in the *New Northwest*, September 26, 1878–May 15, 1879.

From the West to the West (a revised version of *Captain Gray's Company*). Chicago: McClurg, 1905.

"The Happy Home, or the Husband's Triumph." Serialized in the *New Northwest*, November 20, 1874–May 14, 1875.

"Her Lot, or How She Was Protected" (later revised as "Ethel Graeme's Destiny"). Serialized in the *New Northwest*, February 1, 1878–September 19, 1878.

"Judith Reid: A Plain Story of a Plain Woman." Serialized in the *New Northwest*, May 12, 1871–December 22, 1871.

"Laban McShane: A Frontier Story." Serialized in the *New Northwest*, September 13, 1883–March 6, 1884.

"Madge Morrison, the Molalla Maid and Matron." Serialized in the *New Northwest*, December 10, 1875–June 15, 1877.

"Martha Marblehead: The Maid and Matron of Chehalem." Serialized in the *New Northwest*, June 29, 1877–February 8, 1878.

"Mrs. Hardine's Will." Serialized in the *New Northwest*, November 20, 1879–August 26, 1880.

"The Mystery of Castle Rock: A Story of the Pacific Northwest." Serialized in the *New Northwest*, March 2, 1882–September 7, 1882.

"The Old and the New." Serialized in the *Pacific Empire*, January 7, 1897–December 30, 1897.

"One Woman's Sphere, or the Mystery of Eagle Cove." Serialized in the *New Northwest*, June 4, 1875–December 3, 1875.

"Shack-Locks: A Story of the Times." Serialized in the *New Northwest*, October 3, 1895–March 26, 1896.

WORKS BY SUSAN B. ANTHONY

History of Woman Suffrage. Vol. 1 (1881), vol. 2 (1882), vol. 3 (1886). Edited by Susan B. Anthony, Elizabeth Cady Stanton and Matilda Joslyn Gage.

The Life and Work of Susan B. Anthony: A Story of the Evolution of the Status of Women. 1898.

The Revolution (editor), 1868–1870.

Appendix B
Oregon Women's Timeline

1800s

Various Native American tribes occupy the land. "Oregon Territory" or "Oregon Country" comes into existence when the Treaty of 1818 splits the ownership of the area between the United States and Great Britain, and the same year, the western part of the Louisiana Purchase is solidified with Spain.

Women's lives are greatly variant depending on class and income level, but it is clear the presence of women increased steadily in the West during this century. The population of women in the West jumps from 4,949 in 1850 to 20,709 in 1860.[106] Their duties differ also. Women in cities can grow accustomed to purchasing ready-made things more often or hiring out housework, and indeed, it is a mark of class level to be able to do so, especially as the Industrial Revolution begins to roll on.

1844

Catherine Sager, a survivor of a calamitous wagon train journey on the Oregon Trail, outlives both her parents to get to the Whitman Mission. She had become the proxy caretaker as the oldest of her seven siblings to reach the Pacific Northwest. In the mission area, near the border of what now marks the separation between Oregon and Washington State, they are grateful to join the Whitman family and other adopted siblings and share the chores. Some of the things they help with are the washing for the large group, as most women were traditionally in charge of:

Some may ask how the washing for so large a family was managed. As early as 4 o'clock all hands were mustered for work in the kitchen, Mrs. Whitman at the head. Tubs and barrels were put in use, and all the implements needed were at hand. The boys, with long aprons tied around them, brought the water and did the pounding, while the women rubbed the clothes. Jokes were current and all were in good humor. By school time (9 o'clock) the clothes were on the line. It fell to the lot of myself and brother to get breakfast on wash days.[107]

1853
Abigail Scott and family travel on the Oregon Trail as part of a wagon train. It is part of the largest migration west on the Oregon Trail up to that point, in what must have seemed like a never-ending train of over one thousand people that year. Thousands of people signed Emigrant Rock, but historians estimate there were 150,000 people traveling west between 1843 and 1853.

1862
The Homestead Act brings men and women west with much more regularity. Women can own land, as the act states, but are most often prized as a means for men to procure more land for themselves in the free-for-all over all the "unoccupied" land that the United States is trying to rush to claim.

The Homestead Act
May 20, 1862
AN ACT to secure homesteads to actual settlers on the public domain.
Be it enacted, That any person who is the head of a family, or who has arrived at the age of twenty-one years, and is a citizen of the United States, or who shall have filed his declaration of intention to become such, as required by the naturalization laws of the United States, and who has never borne arms against the United States Government or given aid and comfort to its enemies, shall, from and after the first of January, eighteen hundred and sixty-three, be entitled to enter one quarter-section or a less quantity of unappropriated public lands.[108]

1871

Abigail Scott Duniway begins her newspaper "for all peoples," the *New Northwest.* She also accompanies Susan B. Anthony on their trip around the Pacific Northwest to promote women's suffrage.

With their help, the Washington Woman Suffrage Association is formed after the Olympia Women's Suffrage Convention.

1912

Women get the right to vote in Oregon.

Appendix C

National/International Timeline of the History of Women's Rights

Some of this timeline is provided courtesy of the Library of Congress, which compiled it with the aid of researcher E. Susan Barber. I have omitted items not pertinent to my argument and added others, crediting where necessary. My thanks to Ms. Barber and the librarians at the LOC for their gracious permission of the use of portions of this timeline.

1776

Abigail Adams writes to her husband, John, who is attending the Continental Congress in Philadelphia, asking that he and the other men—who were at work on the Declaration of Independence—"Remember the Ladies." John responds with humor. The Declaration's wording specifies that "all men are created equal."

1800s

"In Indiana, the 1880 census reported a population of almost 2 million residents, about 55 per square mile, 1,010,000 men and 968,000 women. About three out of four people lived in rural areas."[109]

1820–1880

Evidence from a variety of printed sources published during this period—advice manuals, poetry and literature, sermons, medical texts—reveals that Americans, in general, hold highly stereotypical notions about women's and men's roles in society. Historians would later term this phenomenon the "Cult of Domesticity."

1837
The first National Female Anti-Slavery Society convention meets in New York City. Lucretia Mott, a Quaker activist, is instrumental in organizing the convention, having had the experience of being denied membership in earlier antislavery organizations because she was a woman.

July 19–20, 1848
The first women's rights convention in the United States is held in Seneca Falls, New York. The idea for the convention arises spontaneously out of a discussion among Lucretia Mott, Elizabeth Cady Stanton and three other women over tea. Many participants sign a "Declaration of Sentiments and Resolutions" that outlines the main issues and goals for the emerging women's movement. Thereafter, women's rights meetings are held on a regular basis.

1866
Elizabeth Cady Stanton and Susan B. Anthony form the American Equal Rights Association, an organization for white and black women and men dedicated to the goal of universal suffrage.

1868
The Fourteenth Amendment is ratified, which extends to all citizens the protections of the Constitution against unjust state laws. This amendment is the first to define "citizens" and "voters" as "male."

1869
The women's rights movement splits into two factions as a result of disagreements over the Fourteenth and soon-to-be-passed Fifteenth Amendments. Elizabeth Cady Stanton and Susan B. Anthony form the more radical, New York–based National Woman Suffrage Association (NWSA). Lucy Stone, Henry Blackwell and Julia Ward Howe organize the more conservative American Woman Suffrage Association (AWSA), which is centered in Boston. In this same year, the Wyoming territory is organized with a women's suffrage provision. In 1890, Wyoming is admitted to the Union with its suffrage provision intact.

1870
The Fifteenth Amendment enfranchises black men. NWSA refuses to work for its ratification, arguing, instead, that it be "scrapped" in favor of

a Sixteenth Amendment providing universal suffrage. Frederick Douglass breaks with Stanton and Anthony over NWSA's position.

1870

The American Woman Suffrage Association begins publishing the *Woman's Journal*, under the editorship of Lucy Stone, Henry Blackwell and Mary A. Livermore (who gives up her own Chicago publication, *The Agitator*, in order to participate in the venture).

1870–1875

Several women—including Virginia Louisa Minor, Victoria Woodhull and Myra Bradwell—attempt to use the Fourteenth Amendment in the courts to secure the vote (Minor and Woodhull) or the right to practice law (Bradwell). They all are unsuccessful.

1871

In Portland, Oregon, Abigail Scott Duniway begins publishing a weekly newspaper, *New Northwest*, dedicated to women's rights and suffrage.

1872

Susan B. Anthony is arrested and brought to trial in Rochester, New York, for attempting to vote for Ulysses S. Grant in the presidential election. At the same time, Sojourner Truth appears at a polling booth in Grand Rapids, Michigan, demanding a ballot; she is turned away.

1874

The Woman's Christian Temperance Union (WCTU) is founded by Annie Wittenmyer. With Frances Willard at its head (1876), the WCTU becomes an important force in the fight for women's suffrage. Not surprisingly, one of the most vehement opponents to women's enfranchisement is the liquor lobby, which fears women might use the franchise to prohibit the sale of liquor.

1876–1879

Lawyer Belva Ann Lockwood is denied permission to practice before the Supreme Court. She spends three years pushing through legislation that enables women to practice before the court and becomes the first woman to do so in 1879.

1878

A Woman Suffrage Amendment is introduced in the United States Congress. The wording is unchanged in 1919, when the amendment finally passes both houses.

1884

In the presidential contest of this year, Belva Ann Lockwood runs for president on the National Equal Rights Party ticket and a reform platform. She wins 4,149 votes in six states.

1890

The NWSA and the AWSA are reunited as the National American Woman Suffrage Association (NAWSA) under the leadership of Elizabeth Cady Stanton. Alice Stone Blackwell, editor of the *Woman's Journal*, an organ of the American Woman Suffrage Association, is instrumental in merging the two groups. During this same year, Jane Addams and Ellen Gates Starr found Hull House, a settlement house project in Chicago's Nineteenth Ward. Within one year, there are more than one hundred settlement houses—largely operated by women—throughout the United States. The settlement house movement and the Progressive campaign of which it is a part propel thousands of college-educated white women and a number of women of color into lifetime careers in social work. It also makes women an important voice to be reckoned with in American politics.

1893

Hannah Greenbaum Solomon founds the National Council of Jewish Women (NCJW) after a meeting of the Jewish Women's Congress at the Columbian Exposition in Chicago, Illinois. In that same year, Colorado becomes the first state to adopt a state amendment enfranchising women. Per author Mary Greene in her book written in 1893, "In Russia, and in all Russian Asia, women who are heads of households vote by proxy at municipal and village elections upon all local questions. (Law of 1870.) In Sweden, for many years, women have voted at local elections, and since 1862 they have had municipal suffrage."[110]

1895

Elizabeth Cady Stanton publishes *The Woman's Bible.* After its publication, NAWSA moves to distance itself from this venerable suffrage pioneer because many conservative suffragists consider her to be too radical and, thus, potentially damaging to the suffrage campaign. From this time, Stanton—who resigned as NAWSA president in 1892—is no longer invited to sit on the stage at NAWSA conventions.

1896

Washington Woman Suffrage Association, Ida B. Wells-Barnett, Margaret Murray Washington, Fanny Jackson Coppin, Frances Ellen Watkins Harper, Charlotte Forten Grimké and former slave Harriet Tubman meet in Washington, D.C., to form the National Association of Colored Women (NACW).

1900

At the age of twenty-nine, Maud Wood Park finds herself the youngest delegate to the NAWSA convention of this year. Working with Inez Haynes Gillmore, she works to attract more young members, establishing what will eventually become the national College Equal Suffrage League. Symbolizing the passing of the suffrage torch to a new generation, Anthony steps down as president of NAWSA. Recognizing Carrie Chapman Catt's potential as an organizer and a speaker, Anthony chooses Catt to succeed her.

March 3, 1913

Members of the Congressional Union organize a suffrage parade, carefully scheduling it for the day before President Wilson's inauguration (it is said that when Wilson arrived in town, he found the streets empty of welcoming crowds and was told that everyone was on Pennsylvania Avenue watching the parade). Not all of the parade observers are suffrage supporters. Hostile members of the crowd swarm and insult the marching women. The publicity resulting from this incident instigates an investigation by District of Columbia Commissioners and provides further momentum for the suffrage campaign.

1914

The National Federation of Women's Clubs—which by this time includes more than two million white women and women of color throughout the United States—formally endorses the suffrage campaign.

1916

NAWSA president Carrie Chapman Catt unveils her "winning plan" for suffrage victory at a convention in Atlantic City, New Jersey. Catt's plan required the coordination of activities by a vast cadre of suffrage workers in both state and local associations.

1916
Jeannette Rankin of Montana becomes the first American woman elected to represent her state in the U.S. House of Representatives.

May–June 1919
The Nineteenth Amendment passes both House and Senate in a special session and heads to the states to be ratified.

August 26, 1920
The Nineteenth Amendment is adopted after being ratified by thirty-six states. Women in the United States have the right to vote.

1920–1921
NAWSA dissolves, but its organization contains the origin of the League of Women Voters. The first president of the league is Maud Wood Park.

1923
The National Woman's Party first proposes the Equal Rights Amendment to eliminate discrimination based on gender. It has never been ratified by all states.

2017
Nevada becomes the thirty-sixth state to ratify the Equal Rights Amendment on March 22, 2017. It is still two states shy of the number needed to pass in the nation.

Notes

Preface

1. Duniway, "Speeches of Abigail Scott Duniway."

Introduction

2. On the Campaign for Divorce Law Reform, 1860.
3. Debs, "Susan B. Anthony."
4. Lake, "She Flies with Her Own Wings."
5. Swindler, "What Would Suffragist Abigail Scott Duniway Think?"
6. Nash, "Abigail V. Harvey."
7. Swindler, "What Would Suffragist Abigail Scott Duniway Think?"

Chapter 1

8. AZQuotes.com, "Duniway."
9. Riddle, "Duniway."
10. Center for the Study of the Pacific Northwest, "Census Data."
11. Merriam, "The 'Other Portland,'" 258–68.
12. Aldrich, "Oregon's First Woman Lawyer," 206.
13. Jimenez, "Red-Lights of Portland," 4, 7.
14. Riddle, "Duniway."

Chapter 2

15. BrainyQuote.com, "Anthony."
16. Center for the Study of the Pacific Northwest, "Lesson Nine: Settlers and Societies."
17. Duniway, "Abigail Scott Duniway, Path Breaker," 202–5.
18. Morrison, *Ladies Were Not Expected.*
19. Wikipedia, "Donation Land Claim Act."
20. Duniway, *Path Breaking*, 45–46.
21. Ibid.
22. Morrison, *Ladies Were Not Expected.*
23. Ibid.
24. Kansas State Historical Society, "Cholera."
25. O'Carroll, "Symphysiotomy Survivors."
26. Rogstad, "Bones of Oregon Trail Pioneers."
27. Flora, "Emigrants to Oregon."
28. Ward and Maveety, *"Yours for Liberty."*
29. Duniway, "Abigail Scott Duniway, Path Breaker."
30. Duniway, *Path Breaking.*
31. Ibid.
32. Ibid.

Chapter 3

33. Notable Quotes, "Susan B. Anthony."
34. Duniway, *Path Breaking.*
35. Ibid., 19.

Chapter 4

36. Notable Quotes, "Susan B. Anthony."
37. Duniway, *Path Breaking.*
38. Silver, "Emily Pitts Stevens."
39. Duniway, "San Francisco County Woman Suffrage Association."
40. Ibid.
41. Duniway, *Path Breaking.*
42. Vorjack, "A Bit More on Virginia Woodhull."

43. Moynihan, *Rebel for Rights*.
44. White, "Lives of Nineteenth-Century American Women," 137–46.
45. Morrison, *Ladies Were Not Expected*.

Chapter 5

46. Notable Quotes, "Susan B. Anthony."
47. National Women Suffrage Association, *Whole World's Temperance Convention*, 10–11.
48. Ibid.
49. Peterson, "Susan Brownwell Anthony."
50. Gordon, "Elizabeth Cady Stanton and Susan B. Anthony Papers Project."
51. National Park Service, "Elizabeth Cady Stanton."
52. Library of Congress, "Elizabeth Cady Stanton and Susan B. Anthony."
53. Susan B. Anthony House, "Susan B. Anthony Timeline."
54. National Park Service, "Elizabeth Cady Stanton."
55. Susan B. Anthony House, "Susan B. Anthony Timeline."
56. AccessibleArchives.com, "The Revolution."
57. Thomas, "Elizabeth Cady Stanton."
58. Susan B. Anthony House, "Susan B. Anthony Timeline."
59. Duniway, *Path Breaking*.
60. Greenspan, "9 Things You Should Know."
61. Donald, "True Soap Opera."

Chapter 6

62. AZQuotes.com, "Duniway."
63. Andrews and Woodhull, "And the Truth Shall Make You Free."
64. Anthony, "Suffrage and the Working Woman," 135–39.
65. Lapham, "Sojourner Truth."

Chapter 7

66. AZQuotes.com, "Duniway."
67. Harper, *Life and Work of Susan B. Anthony*.

68. Duniway, *Path Breaking*.
69. Harper, *Life and Work of Susan B. Anthony*.
70. Ibid.
71. Moynihan, "Of Women's Rights and Freedom," 34.
72. Morrison, *Ladies Were Not Expected*.
73. Ward and Maveety, *"Yours for Liberty."*
74. Stevensen, "Susan B. Anthony Inspires Washington."
75. Harvey, "Salem's Famous Visitors."

Chapter 8

76. Duniway, "Editorial Correspondence."
77. Fields-White, "The Root: How Racism Tainted Women's Suffrage."
78. Anthony, "Susan B. Anthony's Lecture Tour."
79. Moynihan, "Of Women's Rights and Freedom," 34.
80. Duniway, *Path Breaking*.
81. Duniway, "Editorial Proceedings."
82. Stevensen, "Susan B. Anthony Inspires Washington."
83. Andrews, "Susan B. Anthony Addresses Territorial Legislature."
84. Stevensen, "Susan B. Anthony Inspires Washington."

Chapter 9

85. Notable Quotes, "Susan B. Anthony."
86. Anthony, "Susan B. Anthony's Lecture Tour."
87. Duniway, *Path Breaking*.
88. Jensen, "Women Suffrage in Oregon."
89. Mead, *How the Vote Was Won*.
90. Moynihan, *Rebel for Rights*.
91. Duniway, *Path Breaking*
92. Moynihan, "Of Women's Rights and Freedom."
93. Duniway, *Path Breaking*.
94. Moynihan, *Rebel for Rights*.

Chapter 10

95. Notable Quotes, "Susan B. Anthony."
96. Peck, "Susan B. Anthony Dares to Vote!"
97. *United States of America v. Susan B. Anthony*.
98. Ibid.
99. Peck, "Susan B. Anthony Dares to Vote!"
100. Ramos, "Concepts of Ideology."
101. Anthony, World's Congress of Representative Women, 463–66.
102. Mead, *How the Vote Was Won*.
103. Wikipedia, "The Woman's Bible."
104. Cheyney, *People of Purpose*.
105. Biography, "Susan B. Anthony."

Appendix B

106. Duniway, Abigail Scott. "Editorial Correspondence." *New Northwest*, October 22, 1875.
107. Pringle, "Across the Plains in 1844."
108. PBS.org, "Homestead Act."

Appendix C

109. Connor Prairie Interactive History Park
110. Greene, "Legal Condition of Woman."

BIBLIOGRAPHY

AccessibleArchives.com. "The Revolution." Accessed April 1, 2017. www.accessible-archives.com/collections/the-revolution.

Aldrich, Myna. "Oregon's First Woman Lawyer." In *With Her Own Wings*, edited by Helen Krebs Smith, 206. Portland, OR: Beattie and Company, 1948.

Andrews, Mildred. "Susan B. Anthony Addresses Territorial Legislature on October 19, 1871, Then Helps Found Washington Woman Suffrage Association." Historylink.org, September 27, 2003. Accessed May 26, 2017. www.historylink.org/File/5557.

Andrews, Stephen Pearl, and Victoria C. Woodhull. "And the Truth Shall Make You Free: A Speech on the Principles of Social Freedom." The Molinari Institute, November 20, 1871. Accessed April 27, 2017. praxeology.net/SPA-VCW-PSF.htm.

Anthony, Susan B. "Constitutional Argument: Speech After Being Convicted of Voting in the 1872 Presidential Election." Gifts of Speech. Accessed June 8, 2017. gos.sbc.edu/a/anthony.html.

———. "Suffrage and the Working Woman—1871." In *Elizabeth Cady Stanton, Susan B. Anthony, Correspondence, Writings, Speeches*, by Ellen DuBois, 135–39. New York: Schocken Books, Inc., 1998.

———. "Women in Oregon: Susan B. Anthony's Lecture Tour of Oregon, Washington Territory, and Victoria, B.C., September, October, November 1871." Lewis & Clark Digital Collections. Accessed March 29, 2017. digitalcollections.lclark.edu/exhibits/show/a-guide-to-digital-resources-f/susan-b--anthony-s-visits-to-o/part-i--1871.

———. *The World's Congress of Representative Women*. Chicago: Rand McNally & Company, 1893, 463–66.

AZQuotes.com. "Abigail Scott Duniway Quotes." Accessed June 8, 2017. www.azquotes.com/author/26063-Abigail_Scott_Duniway.

Biography. "Susan B. Anthony." April 27, 2017. Accessed June 7, 2017. www.biography.com/people/susan-b-anthony-194905.

Center for the Study of the Pacific Northwest. "Census Data for Oregon and California, 1850 and 1860." University of Washington. Accessed February 7, 2017. www.washington.edu/uwired/outreach/cspn/Website/Classroom%20Materials/Pacific%20Northwest%20History/Lessons/Lesson%209/Census%20Data.html.

———. "Lesson Nine: Settlers and Societies in California and Oregon." University of Washington. Accessed February 11, 2017. www.washington.edu/uwired/outreach/cspn/Website/Classroom%20Materials/Pacific%20Northwest%20History/Lessons/Lesson%209/9.html.

Cheyney, Arnold. *People of Purpose*. N.p.: Good Year Books, 1998.

Conner Prairie. "Lives of Women." N.d. Accessed November 10, 2017. www.connerprairie.org/education-research/indiana-history-1860-1900/lives-of-women.

Debs, Eugene V. "Susan B. Anthony: A Reminiscence." www.marxists.org, January 1909. Accessed June 8, 2017. www.marxists.org/archive/debs/works/1909/1909-anthony.htm.

Donald, David Herbert. "True Soap Opera." *New York Times*, January 30, 2000.

Duniway, Abigail Scott. "Editorial Correspondence." *New Northwest*, October 22, 1875, Image 2.

———. "Editorial Proceedings, Olympia, Washington." *New Northwest*, October 23, 1871, 2. www.washingtonhistory.org/files/library/AnthonysSpeech.pdf.

———. *Path Breaking*. New York: Shocken Books, 1871.

———. "San Francisco County Woman Suffrage Association." *The Pioneer*, January 5, 1871.

———. "The Speeches of Abigail Scott Duniway." *She Flies with Her Own Wings*, October 7, 2011. Accessed June 8, 2017. asduniway.org/wp-content/uploads/2010/11/DESTINY74.ASD-Edits.pdf.

Duniway, David. "Abigail Scott Duniway, Path Breaker." In *With Her Own Wings*, edited by Helen Krebs Smith, 202–5. Portland, OR: Beattie and Company, 1948.

EqualRightsAmendment.org. "The Equal Rights Amendment: Unfinished Business for the Constitution." 1999. Accessed June 9, 2017. www.equalrightsamendment.org/states.htm#NV.

Fields-White, Monee. "The Root: How Racism Tainted Women's Suffrage." National Public Radio, March 25, 2011. Accessed June 9, 2017. www.npr.org/2011/03/25/134849480/the-root-how-racism-tainted-womens-suffrage.

Flora, Stephanie, comp. "Emigrants to Oregon in 1852." OregonPioneers.com, 2009. Accessed August 18, 2017. www.oregonpioneers.com/1852_RZ.htm.

Gordon, Ann D., ed. "The Elizabeth Cady Stanton and Susan B. Anthony Papers Project." 1997. Accessed March 30, 2017.

Greene, Miss Mary. "Legal Condition of Woman in 1492–1892." A Celebration of Women Writers. UPenn.edu Digital Library, 1894. Accessed February 7, 2017. digital.library.upenn.edu/women/eagle/congress/greene.html.

Greenspan, Jesse. "9 Things You Should Know About Victoria Woodhull." History.com, September 23, 2013. Accessed April 4, 2017. www.history.com/news/9-things-you-should-know-about-victoria-woodhull.

Harper, Ida Hustead. *The Life and Work of Susan B. Anthony: Including Public Addresses, Her Own Letters and Many from Her Contemporaries During Fifty Years.* Vol. 1. New York: Bowen-Merrill Company, 1898.

Harvey, Cynthia. "Salem's Famous Visitors." SalemHistory.net. Accessed May 19, 2017. www.salemhistory.net/people/famous_visitors.htm.

Jensen, Kimberly. "Women Suffrage in Oregon." Oregon Encyclopedia, October 17, 2014. Accessed May 28, 2017. oregonencyclopedia.org/articles/woman_suffrage_in_oregon/#.WSreo1gzrIU.

Jimenez, Corri. "The Red-Lights of Portland." *Associated Students for Historic Preservation Journal* 4, no. 7 (Winter 1997). Accessed February 11, 2017. pages.uoregon.edu/ashp/Journal/1997_Winter.pdf.

Kansas State Historical Society. "Cholera." June 2003. Accessed February 15, 2017. www.kshs.org/kansapedia/cholera/12010.

Lake, Randall A. 2011. "She Flies with Her Own Wings." October 7, 2011. Accessed June 8, 2017. asduniway.org.

Lapham, Thea Rozetta. "Sojourner Truth: A Life Led by Faith." 1997. Accessed August 18, 2017. www.sojournertruth.org/Library/Archive/LifeLedByFaith.htm.

Library of Congress. "Elizabeth Cady Stanton and Susan B. Anthony." AmericasLibrary.gov. Accessed April 6, 2017. www.americaslibrary.gov/aa/stanton/aa_stanton_friends_2.html.

Mead, Rebecca J. *How the Vote Was Won: Women Suffrage in the Western United States, 1868–1914.* New York: New York University, 2004.

Merriam, Paul G. "The 'Other Portland': A Statistical Note on Foreign-Born, 1860–1910." *Oregon Historical Quarterly* (1979): 258–68. Accessed February 11, 2017. www.jstor.org/stable/i20613677.

Morrison, Dorothy N. *Ladies Were Not Expected.* New York: Atheneum, 1977.

Moynihan, Ruth Barnes. "Of Women's Rights and Freedom: Abigail Scott Duniway." In *Women in Pacific Northwest History: Revised Edition*, by Karen J. Blair, 34. Seattle: University of Washington Press, 2014.

———. *Rebel for Rights: Abigail Scott Duniway.* New Haven, CT: Yale University Press, 1983.

Nash, Lee. "Abigail V. Harvey." *Truth's Bright Embrace: Essays and Poems in Honor of Arthur O. Robert.* January 17, 1996.

National Park Service. "Elizabeth Cady Stanton." Accessed April 1, 2017. www.nps.gov/wori/learn/historyculture/elizabeth-cady-stanton.htm.

National Women Suffrage Association. *Whole World's Temperance Convention.* New York: Fowlers and Wells, 1853, 10–11.

Notable Quotes. "Susan B. Anthony." Notable-quotes.com.

O'Carroll, Sinead. "Symphysiotomy Survivors Gather to Recount Stories of Torture." Journal.ie, November 14, 2012. Accessed February 15, 2017. jrnl.ie/673113.

PBS.org. "The Homestead Act: May 20, 1862." Archives of the West. Accessed February 7, 2017. www.pbs.org/weta/thewest/resources/archives/five/homestd.htm.

Peck, Ira. "Susan B. Anthony Dares to Vote!" Scholastic, March 10, 1989. Accessed June 8, 2017. www.scholastic.com/browse/article.jsp?id=4973.

Peterson, Cheyenne. "Susan Brownwell Anthony." Accessed March 30, 2017. susanbrownwellanthony.weebly.com/index.html.

Pettinger, Tejvan. "Susan B. Anthony." Accessed August 10, 2017. https://www.biographyonline.net/women/susan-b-anthony.html.

Pringle, Catherine Sager. "Across the Plains in 1844." PBS.org, circa 1860. Accessed February 7, 2017. www.pbs.org/weta/thewest/resources/archives/two/sager1.htm.

Ramos, Valeriano, Jr. "The Concepts of Ideology, Hegemony, and Organic Intellectuals in Gramsci's Marxism." Marxists.org, March–April 1982. Accessed June 9, 2017. www.marxists.org/history/erol/periodicals/theoretical-review/1982301.htm.

Riddle, Margaret. "Duniway, Abigail Scott (1834–1915)." HistoryLink.org, August 10, 2008. Accessed February 7, 2017. www.historylink.org/File/8720.

Rogstad, Jodi. "Bones of Oregon Trail Pioneers Being Laid to Rest on Ranch Near Glendo." *Wyoming News*, April 27, 2015. Accessed February 15, 2017.

www.wyomingnews.com/things_to_do/bones-of-oregon-trail-pioneers-being-laid-to-rest-on/article_14df318d-ef39-5789-95df-22b297a8262e.html.

Silver, Mae. "Emily Pitts Stevens." FoundSF, San Francisco's Digital Archive. Accessed March 2, 2017. www.foundsf.org/index.php?title=Emily_Pitts_Stevens.

Stevensen, Shanna. "Susan B. Anthony Inspires Washington." Washington Historical Society. Accessed April 30, 2017. www.washingtonhistory.org/files/library/SusanBAnthonyInspiresWashington.pdf.

Susan B. Anthony House. "Susan B. Anthony Timeline." 2013. Accessed April 1, 2017. susanbanthonyhouse.org/timeline.php.

Swindler, Samantha. "What Would Oregon Suffragist Abigail Scott Duniway Think?" *The Oregonian/Oregon Live*, November 8, 2016.

Thomas, J.D. "Elizabeth Cady Stanton: Saving Our Young Girls." Accesible Archives, September 29, 2016. Accessed April 4, 2017. www.accessible-archives.com/2016/09/elizabeth-cady-stanton-saving-young-girls.

The United States of America v. Susan B. Anthony. United States Circuit Court. Northern Disctrict of New York, June 17–18, 1873.

Vorjack. "A Bit More on Virginia Woodhull." Unreasonable Faith, February 27, 2012. Accessed April 27, 2017. www.patheos.com/blogs/unreasonablefaith/2012/02/a-bit-more-on-victoria-woodhull/.

Ward, Jean M., and Elaine A. Maveety, eds. *"Yours for Liberty": Selections from Abigail Scott Duniway's Suffrage Newspaper.* Corvallis: Oregon State University Press, 2000.

White, Barbara. "The Lives of Nineteenth-Century American Women." *NWSA Journal* 15, no. 1 (2003): 137–46.

Wikipedia. "Donation Land Claim Act." September 20, 2016. Accessed February 14, 2017. en.wikipedia.org/wiki/Donation_Land_Claim_Act.

———. "The Woman's Bible." February 13, 2017. Accessed June 7, 2017. en.wikipedia.org/wiki/The_Woman%27s_Bible.

Index

About the Author

By Millie Carpenter

Jennifer Chambers writes about strong women with bold stories. She is a nationally known public speaker on topics like self-advocacy, body love and how the legacies of strong women in history contribute to activism today. Chambers attended the University of Iowa Summer Writing Festival. The co-owner and contributing editor of Groundwaters Publishing, she is a survivor of traumatic brain injury, which forced her to relearn everything from walking and talking to tying her shoes. She lives with her family in the Pacific Northwest and is learning to play bluegrass and Motown on her ukulele—but not at the same time. Her life is fueled by coffee, family, music and books. For booking or signing schedule, contact her website, www.jenniferbyerschambers.com.